The Gift of Language

Library of Jewish Philosophy

The Gift of Language

*Memory and Promise in Adorno,
Benjamin, Heidegger, and Rosenzweig*

ALEXANDER GARCÍA DÜTTMANN

Translated from the French by ARLINE LYONS

Syracuse University Press

Published in the United States of America by Syracuse University
Press, Syracuse, New York 13244-5160, by arrangement with
The Athlone Press, London

First published in French as *La parole donnée memoire et promesse*.
Copyright © 1989 by Editions Galilée

Library of Congress Cataloging-in-Publication Data

García Düttmann, Alexander.
   [Parole donnée. English]
   The gift of language : memory and promise in Adorno, Benjamin,
Heidegger, and Rosenzweig / Alexander García Düttmann; translated from
the French by Arline Lyons.
     p. cm. — (Library of Jewish philosophy)
   Includes bibliographical references and index.
  · ISBN 0-8156-2866-8 (alk. paper) — ISBN 0-8156-2867-6 (pbk. : alk.
paper)
    1. Philosophy. 2. Language and languages — Philosophy. I. Title.
II.Series.

B77.G27 2000
121'.68—dc21

00-039475

This edition is for sale only in North America

Manufactured in Great Britain

For Jacques Derrida

Contents

Note on the English translation

The Gift of Language is my first book, written between 1986 and 1988. Ten years later, and after having tried to develop some of its themes or motifs in *Das Gedächtnis des Denkens. Versuch über Heidegger und Adorno* (*The Memory of Thought: An Essay on Heidegger and Adorno*, Athlone 2001), I believe that its strength, if it has any, is inseparable from its often elliptical character. This is the reason why I have made only a few changes to the original text.

A.G.D.
London

Translator's Note

Existing English translations have been used wherever possible, and modified where necessary by the author. Many thanks to the staff of the British Library, Warwick University Library, University College London Library, Middlesex University Library and Senate House Library.

In the eyes of the cabbalists, it is because
of the name present in it that language
can be spoken.

(Gershom Sholem)

Nothing links man to language better
than his name.

(Walter Benjamin)

Constellations

In *Negative Dialectics*, Adorno says that language is more than a system of signs at the disposal of cognitive functions. Where it is essentially language, before or beyond the system and the sign, it becomes presentation or representation (*Darstellung*) and does not define its concepts. This does not mean that the thinking which Adorno calls negative dialectics, the intent of which is precisely not to be without language ('Hegelian dialectics was a dialectic without language'), renounces definition, quite the opposite: 'A thought which in its own unfolding would not be capable of defining its object, a thought which would not let the thing itself appear intermittently by using the most concise language, would probably be as sterile as a thought gorged with verbal definitions.' *Darstellung* is language as constellation or configuration. It is in no way the representation of a sublating movement which reaches a result. Language designates here the non-negative other of speculation. By definition, a constellation entails the chance of an apparition. Something allows itself to be thought through a constellation, something provokes thought in a constellation. But what is it that appears in the apparition? According to Adorno, the name presents itself as the 'linguistic' prototype of thought without being thought itself: it is the prototype 'at the cost of [the] cognitive function'. In other words, there is no immediate relation to the name for knowledge. The name appears only in a constellation of concepts. Thus, the constellation, language as constellation, is necessary. Thought is unable to name except by placing itself in a constellation, by travelling the path that separates it from the name. This path is the path of *Darstellung*. In *The Jargon of Authenticity*, Adorno denounces (philosophical) language which denies the constellation and tries to name the name in an unthinkable immediacy. (Philosophical) language becomes *jargon* when it claims to be able to denominate without division. A definition takes the name's place and marks the distance between name and concept. The constellation, the necessity of a *Darstellung* which neither refuses definition nor reduces itself to a definition, is a sign of loss: the unity of the name and knowledge, knowledge through the name, the cognising name that Benjamin speaks of, have been lost. The name appears, but its apparition is inseparable from the dispersion that all constellations presuppose. And what if the apparition of the name were nothing other than the gift of language, the memory and promise of that gift? What if the constellation were implicated in the very structure of the gift, thus transforming itself into a plural constellation, into a multiplicity of constellations whose number would not be limited beforehand by a horizon? What if the *Darstellung* in the sense of a constellation or a configurational language were originary?

At the end of his essay on the question of technology, Heidegger speaks of a 'constellation of truth'. Concealment and unconcealment take place or come to pass as a constellation or in a constellation. The question is, therefore, the 'question of the constellation'. It is the saying of art, the saying of the poet – *techné, poiesis* – which speaks the truth, the constellation itself. And this saying only seeks to find the ever obscure name, as Heidegger maintains in his interpretation of Hölderlin, '*Das Gedicht*'. Thus the name, in its very obscurity, is the constellation of truth.

Benjamin defines truth as configuration, as a timeless constellation of ideas which, through concepts, divides and groups phenomena. Ideas are of the order of language: they 'are displayed, without intention, in the act of naming, and they have to be renewed in philosophical contemplation. In this renewal the primordial mode of apprehending words is restored' (*The Origin of German Tragic Drama*). The relation to truth is also, and primarily, 'without intention'. In this way philosophical restitution, the restitution of truth, the *Darstellung* of the idea, manifests itself in an anamnesis which gives the word its proper power of denomination. Later, in his theses on the philosophy of history, Benjamin takes up once again the concept of a constellation in order to point to the stopping of thought (*Stillstellung des Denkens*) which allows the messianic trace in time and history to be grasped: that is to say, the trace of a restored language, of the language of names, of the name itself. The messianic world is the world in which language is shared absolutely and all translation is complete.

Isn't Rosenzweig's star, which makes its way, or which moves in an orbit, a constellation? Isn't it a constellation in its very unity, in the unity of its form or figure, since access to its truth is redoubled, since there is more than one uprooting, more than one displacement, more than one tearing away from a place (*Entortung*)? In a text on Rosenzweig entitled 'Straying Root', Massimo Cacciari contrasts the authentic *Entortung* which defines Judaism with the global *Entortung* which characterises the crisis of the *nomos*: 'the path, the way of the destruction of the *nomos* is the meaning of Europe or of Christianity.'[1] Isn't the name as 'absolutely gathered speech' or 'absolute gathering of speech' found inside a star affected by a certain exteriority? Doesn't it stand in the constellation of a double access, in the Judeo-Christian constellation?

Adorno, Benjamin, Heidegger, Rosenzweig: despite the undeniable differences which constitute the philosophical and historical singularity of each of these thinkers and the challenge of their thought, they have all thought – thought – on the grounds of the name, the apparition of the name as the experience of a constellation.

We can then imagine the impossible dialogue between those who hold such a view of thought and language and those who think the relation to the name completely differently; Wittgenstein or Kripke, for example.[2] How can we decipher this constellation? If we keep to the *Philosophical Investigations*, it is not too difficult to anticipate a Wittgensteinian counter-argument: those who treat the name as something which does not simply lend itself to an analysis of the usage of language or to a formal linguistic analysis would be accused of contributing to a glorification (*Feier*) of language and of creating, not solving, philosophical problems. The ones thus accused would probably reply saying: everything that you attempt to demonstrate with such rigour is certainly pertinent, but you are forgetting the originary experience of language, you remain at the level of a 'conventional theory of language' without thinking the conditions of possibility of that theory, the passage from one level to another. The tales about the apparition of the name are probably fictions, but that doesn't matter. What really interests us is the structural necessity of those tales ... And how can you not glorify an apparition, even if it is terrifying? You do not experience the name, the gift of language, always singular, always to be remembered. You start out from a hypothesis which is subsequently proven, you oppose one hypothesis to another, but we give you our word: that's not all, there's something completely different ...

The four chapters of this book[3] perhaps form a constellation: they can be read separately. Here and there they refer back to one another; the motifs one can distinguish in them intersect while remaining singular. The mark of a certain discontinuity which is the very origin of the constellation has not been erased after the fact.

I

On the Path towards Sacred Names

> In the widest sense, 'to call' means
> to set in motion, to get something underway.
> (Martin Heidegger)[5]

Heidegger and Rosenzweig

What is the 'logic' of the answers that Rosenzweig and Heidegger give, each in a different way and perhaps also while following different paths – or something other than a path – to the question: what is a path?

In a passage from his text on Rosenzweig and Heidegger from 1942–3 ('Heidegger und Rosenzweig. Ein Nachtrag zu "Sein und Zeit"'), Karl Löwith broadly indicates what it is that links and separates these two thinkers. It is their relation to theology. Löwith first quotes from Rosenzweig: 'Theological problems must be translated into human terms and human problems must be pressed until they reach the domain of theology.' He then comments on the quote: 'This characterisation of the "new thinking" applies as much to the thinking of the early Heidegger as it does to Rosenzweig, even if Heidegger's relation to Christianity consists of a turning away (*Abkehrung*) and Rosenzweig's relation to Judaism consists of a return (*Rückkehr*).'[6] So Heidegger – like Rosenzweig – supposedly distanced himself from Christianity. But for what reason? Should he have returned to religion, to theology, to a new thought of the sacred or of the holy which might be associated, in some way, with Judaism? Should he have turned towards eternity, towards something which is not simply temporal, towards something which, for Rosenzweig, is essentially Jewish? This is not only what Löwith suggests in the concluding remarks of his essay by raising the question of that which necessarily exceeds the radical temporality of truth, but also what his statement seems to imply in its very structure, despite its air of objectivity – despite the effect produced by reading it which makes the sentence appear to be a simple constative proposition implying neither evaluation nor criticism. It follows a quote which says that it is not enough to translate theological terms into secular ones. The task of translating them again must be completed, the task of translating man's problems into theological ones. Rosenzweig speaks here only once of translation. Is pressing man's problems to the point at which they become theological problems the same as translating them again? But even if this were the case, the question arises of whether what 'theology' means – what it means according to Rosenzweig and Löwith – is compatible with the Jewish thought of the sacred or of the holy. To the extent that Rosenzweig's statement characterises the 'new thinking', nothing can prevent us from analysing the conclusion Löwith draws from it, a conclusion concerning the relationship between Rosenzweig and Heidegger or their non-relation to each other in their relation to theology, as a requirement. In any event, Löwith makes it clear in his autobiography *My Life in Germany Before and After 1933* that Heidegger was enough of a theologian to know what he was doing when he refused to speak of the Good Lord and defined death as 'an "insurmountable instance" of our Being and our potentiality-for-Being',[7] thus translating what needed to be translated. However, if he was still translating he hadn't really renounced theology. In his autobiography, Löwith calls this theology a 'godless theology', an 'atheist theology', an 'impious theology' (*gottlose Theologie*). The question then is whether Heidegger, while being enough of a theologian not to be one, was still enough of a theologian to address man's essence, which according to Rosenzweig is more proper to man than the propriety revealed by a translation into secular terms. On the subject of death, Löwith writes:

> In opposing the thought of philosophy which flees death, Rosenzweig chooses a fundamental presupposition as his starting point: that life is destined to end in death; Heidegger chooses the same point of departure [...] There is also an essential difference between the two thoughts linked together

by this common trait. On the one hand, Rosenzweig advances along a path leading him to 'eternal life', passing through Creation as beginning, Revelation as middle and Redemption as end; an 'eternal truth', the star, corresponds to 'eternal life'. On the other hand, Heidegger describes belief in eternal truth as a residue of Christian theology, something which has not yet been radically eliminated.[8]

Heidegger was perhaps still too much of a Christian to grasp the implications of the 'eternal truth' of the star which must shine 'in the innermost constriction of the Jewish heart'.[9] If Heidegger turned his back on Christianity because he was a theologian at heart, Rosenzweig was even more of a theologian, since he returned to Judaism.

Löwith's commentary makes sense only on the basis of this requirement: *there must be a return*. In other words: turning away isn't enough, there can be no turning away without a return. Hence these questions. What does it mean to turn away from Christianity, from religion, from theology? What does it mean to turn towards Judaism? Where do this turning away and this returning intersect with the question of the path? More succinctly, what do they require, what does their interlacing require, the interlacing which ties them together and at the same time ties them to the question of the path – and maybe also to that of the name, the sacred name?

When discussing Rosenzweig's and Heidegger's thought, we must locate the question of the path in what we may call the *sacred*, even if further distinctions reveal themselves to be necessary. This may be difficult to conceive when we speak of Heidegger, but a late text which addresses the question of the path is actually called 'The Want of Sacred Names' (*'Der Fehl heiliger Namen'*). I will lay out, fairly schematically, three features that seem to me to be common to Rosenzweig's and Heidegger's thought.

(1) Heidegger's turning away – is it really a turning away? – also presents itself as a return or as a step backwards which brings us to a hidden or forgotten origin. We see an analogous gesture in Rosenzweig and Heidegger; for the latter the path (*Weg*), what must be thought, thought itself, is closer to the origin than the method which prevents us from noticing 'the

character of thought as way'.[10] It is certainly a strange origin: it must be invented, one returns to it by inventing it, given that it cannot express itself – according to Heidegger – unless it expresses itself in Greek, this language where it is nowhere to be found. For the former, Rosenzweig, the path as eternal way (*ewiger Weg*) is the way of Christianity where the Christian community attests to itself (*bezeugen*) by attesting to it; that is to say, by speaking, by becoming a community of missionaries who are gifted with eloquence. This eternal way not only accompanies the eternal life of the Jewish people (an eternity that doubles the other eternity) but also opposes that life. The way, as I will attempt to demonstrate, remains secondary in relation to the immediacy (*Unmittelbarkeit*) characteristic of eternal life. This immediacy does not need words. It passes, without mediation, into the name, into its silence. The path, the way: one word more, one word too many.

(2) Thinking the path becomes unavoidable for Heidegger when he experiences a lack: the want of sacred names. This experience is experience itself, the 'field-path' (*Wegfeld*).[11] Why does Heidegger take up Hölderlin's line '*the sacred names are wanting*', one that refers to sacred names and that belongs to an elegy whose title ('*Heimkunft*') names a return? He quotes it at the moment when he wants to point out that experiencing, the experiencing of experience, cannot be done except while on the path, *unterwegs*. The essence of experience or of the path is lost when it is identified with method, with the dialectical movement of the concept which is the truth of method. This causes the alienation (*Entfremdung*) of the immediate, of what has not yet been experienced (*das Unerfahrene*). It is in this way that the immediate can return (*zurückgehen*) and present itself in its reality and ultimate truth: as the property (*Eigentum*) of consciousness. At the end of the chapter 'The Rays or the Eternal Way', which can be found in the middle of the third part of *The Star of Redemption*, Rosenzweig writes:

> It is experience come home (*Heimkehr*) [...], the verification of verity. The truth lies behind the way. The way ends where home has been reached. For though its end lies in eternity, and it is thus eternal, it is at the same time finite, since eternity is its end. Where everything is on fire, there

are no more rays, there is only one light. There 'the earth shall be full of the knowledge of the Lord as the waters cover the sea'. In the ocean of light every way is submerged like vanity. But thou, oh God, art truth.[12]

The eternity of truth, of this truth pronounced here, at the end, through an apostrophe, without name, is still other than the double eternity of way and life, eternities that are finite but not symmetrical, not symmetrical because they are finite; before the Eternal, before truth, all ways fade away; 'Of a truth, within truth, life too disappears.' The goal of the thought of the eternal way and eternal life is eternity as the beyond of the name: "The end, however, is nameless; it is above any name. The very sanctification of the name occurs only so that the name might one day be muted. Beyond the word – and what is the name but the collective word – beyond the word there shines silence."[13] There would be no eternal life if the name that will be muted, the name above any name, the name 'outliving and more-than-living', the 'one name al(l)-one' (*der eine Name all-ein*), was not wanting.

(3) Experience understood as a path to be travelled, as the experience of a lack, of a want of sacred names, of a want of the 'one name al(l)-one' (but we must not be too hasty in placing these experiences at the level of the same experience); experience understood as a return to the Greek, or to the eternity of truth to which Jewish people accede more easily, since their relationship to eternity is a more immediate relationship – such experience is an experience of the future. Something emerged, something happened (Greek thought, revelation) which has yet to emerge, to happen so that we can say: it emerged, it happened. What has taken place thus appeals to an event to come. For Heidegger, it is the reinvention of what had not been said in Greek and what cannot be said except in Greek – can it be said in German? Why doesn't Heidegger say it in German? For Rosenzweig, it is redemption.

These are the three features common to Rosenzweig and Heidegger's thought of the path. In both cases, a detour imposes itself and precedes the return, on the one hand to an origin, on the other to an immediacy. For both, the return takes the form of a relation of experience to the name. In both cases a future must be awaited which points to an event belonging and not belonging to the past – which explains the possibility of the detour.

I

The immediate: frontier, limit and definition

The chapter that Rosenzweig devotes to the eternal way opens with the following sentence: 'No man has the power to grasp the thought of the Creator for "his ways are not our ways and his thoughts are not our thoughts".'[14] Rosenzweig thus starts by quoting and commenting on Maimonides, who says that there are some ways which remain forbidden to us, the ways of divine thought. Maybe we should add: if we speak of divine ways, it is because we are experiencing the way, and because it is this very experience we undergo in the first place. This is true of us, the Jews, but also, in another sense, of us, the Christians. We must be extremely careful, for the truth of the 'eternal way' as the truth of the Christian community remains external to those who affirm: 'Our life is no longer meshed with anything outside ourselves. We have struck root in ourselves.' It remains untrue with respect to this self-rooted life, it seems alien to the Jewish people which, for this reason, is always found everywhere. It is found anywhere, on all paths and ways, but without being found there. Because it is here and elsewhere, because it is nowhere, this people is the only one to know distances and real frontiers, for example, when it is a question of war. Rosenzweig gives only this example, as if to understand the meaning of a distance and of a frontier which keeps the other at a distance, it were necessary to understand war, its internal divisions or splits:

> In keeping with the spirit of Christianity, which admits of no boundaries, there are for it [the people of the Christian era, A.G.D.] no 'very distant' peoples [it is against these peoples that the Jews wage war 'according to the universal rules of martial law', A.G.D.]. Holy War and political war, which in Jewish law were constitutionally distinguished, are here

blended into one. Precisely because they are not really God's people and are still only in process (*auf dem Weg*) of so becoming, they cannot draw this fine distinction; they simply cannot know to which extent a war is a holy war, and to which extent merely a secular war.[15]

Let us note this implicit definition: the eternal way is a way of becoming and, in consequence, the sign of a want, of a lack, of an immediacy which is lacking. Compared with the eternity of Jewish life the eternity of the way is an eternal becoming, a becoming eternal within eternity itself. Eternal life itself must become the eternity of an out-living, of a life more living than the life of survivors: 'There is eternal life only in contrast to the life of those who pave the eternal way' [*Bahner*: this word refers more to those who are clearing, opening or charting a path or a way, A.G.D.]. So the eternal way is this becoming that eternal life has never known and will never know. There are reasons for becoming Christian, for becoming something which becomes, which is not yet 'really God's people', but there is no reason to become Jewish, since one is either Jewish or one is not, in an immediacy which precedes the time of the way. Jewish 'reason' is to be sought in an 'attestation' (*Bezeugung*) which is produced through 'generation' (*Zeugung*) and thus not through the propagation of the word or in the growth of the community united by the word: 'But the people remains the eternal people. The meaning of its life in time is that the years come and go, one after the other as a sequence of waiting, or perhaps wandering, but not of growth.'[16] I will not linger on the motif of waiting (*Warten*): in his discussion of releasement, Heidegger says that waiting constitutes the essence of thought, and he makes it clear that it is a question of waiting and not expectation (*Erwartung*). For the Jewish people and only for them attestation is immediately and essentially generation, since generation is essentially and immediately attestation. Attestation is Jewish, and not only because all attestation, through its legacy-like structure, is a regeneration, a revival of the name (the promise passes through the name, the promised name is the origin of attestation: 'the name of the ancestor is regenerated through the engendered grandson'). An attestation requires a certain immediacy; it is a sort of immediate memory. If I need a long speech to attest to my identity, I am immediately suspect. Just one word (one name) is enough for the Jews, and it is perhaps this self-sufficiency with its implied superiority that makes them even more suspect, which attracts suspicion. The immediacy of an attestation is absolute, lost, ungraspable, as if the attestation annulled that to which it attested the moment it transformed it into something purely attesting: the pure fact of my existence, of my procreation, of being named and naming attests to my being chosen. What is at stake here is the insane certainty of an attestation. Isn't extermination, from this perspective, the radical calling into question of Jewish attestation, the only possible questioning? Can an attempt to uproot the very people that has taken root in itself thanks to the *Bezeugung* be anything other than an extermination? Isn't anti-Semitism, the 'hatred of the Jews', another attestation to the 'stalwart and undeniable vitality of the Jewish people'? Isn't the exterminated people more living than ever?

> Had the Jews of the Old Testament disappeared from the earth like Christ, they would [now] denote the idea of the People, and Zion the idea of the Centre of the World, just as Christ denotes the idea of Man. But the stalwart, undeniable vitality of the Jewish people, attested in the very hatred of the Jews, resists such 'idealising'. Whether Christ is more than an idea – no Christian can know it. But that Israel is more than an idea, that he knows, that he can see. For we live. We are eternal, not as an idea may be eternal; if we are eternal, it is in full reality.[17]

Extermination, we could say, allowing ourselves to be guided by the main thread of this interpretation, operates an idealisation of Judaism which testifies to its opposition to idealism. When absolute attestation has been absolutely called into question, a remainder – not an idea, not even an existence – still refers to the attestation: 'In Judaism, man is always somehow a remnant. He is always somehow a survivor, an inner something, whose exterior was seized by the current of the world and carried off while he himself, what is left of him, remains standing on the shore. Something within him is waiting.'[18] Neither simply immediate nor simply non-immediate, attestation (immediate attestation for the Jews, non-immediate attestation for the Christians) is without measure; but nothing is more dispropor-tionate than this immediacy which assures and precedes verbal attestation.

Silence is the truth of speech and of the name: 'nothing is more essentially Jewish in the deepest sense than a profound distrust of the power of the word and a fervent belief in the power of silence.'[19] In remaining silent, or at least wary of discourse, the Jew keeps himself at the very heart of language, of what others have at their disposal in order to attest to their identity. All languages are at the Jew's disposal, but the Jewish people do not have a language in the way that a particular people has something that would disappear the day no trace of that people remained. The Jew *is* language, he *is* the name: for this 'reason' each Jewish generation is, as such, an attestation to the name. This 'reason' which is not a reason, which is much more and much less than a reason, does not lend itself to dialec-tical or dialectical-speculative formalisation. It opposes a philo-sophical history which claims to be true with respect to a mere general or a reflective history; it opposes it without doing so, it exceeds it. 'There are two sides to every boundary', Rosenz-weig notes.

> By setting borders for ourselves, we border on something else. By being an individual people, a nation becomes a people among others. To close oneself off is to come close to another. But this does not hold when a people refuses to be merely an individual people and wants to be 'the one people'. Under these circumstances it must not close itself off within borders, but include within itself such borders as would, through their double function, tend to make it one individual people among others.[20]

Rosenzweig describes the dialectic of inclusion and exclusion, the dialectic of the frontier, of the limit; he describes an inclu-sion which excludes inclusion in the dialectic Hegel renders as follows: 'Something (*Etwas*) as an immediate determinate being, is, therefore, the limit relative to another something (*anderes Etwas*), but the limit is present in the something itself, which is a something through the mediation of the limit, which is just as much its non-being. Limit is the mediation through which something and something other (*Etwas und Anderes*) each as well is, as is not.'[21] The people which is no longer an individual people, which is 'the only people' – the only people to deserve this name – is the only people to 'know' what a war is, and also the only one which knows nothing of it, the only one to stand beyond the opposition which limits and which allows the limit to be crossed: 'The Jewish people is beyond the contradiction that constitutes the vital drive in the life of the nations – the contradiction between national characteristics and world history [Rosenzweig appears to translate the Hegelian terms *Volksgeist* and *Weltgeist* by those of *Eigenart* and *Weltgeschichte*, A.G.D.], home and faith, earth and heaven – it knows nothing of war.'[22]

I will digress for a moment and add another quote. In 1939–40, Max Horkheimer wrote a very short text entitled *The Jewish Character*.[23] In this piece Horkheimer, the exiled Jew, states that the Jews deny their 'lack of experience'. And the reader asks himself: is there a link between this lack, the denial of the lack and what was happening at that time to Jews in Germany, to German Jews? The mission (*Sendung*) of the Jewish people is meant to rest on a 'lack of experience': by denying their 'lack of experience', the Jews deny their mission. According to Horkheimer, an onto-typological contradiction can be discerned here, a contradiction that divides the 'stamp' (Prägung): the 'historical stamp' (the experience resulting from a denial of an essential lack) must be separated from the 'individual stamp' (the stamp of the Jew who holds himself beyond or at the limit of history, the stamp of the mission which delimits history). This contradiction gives rise to a denial, it is the locus of a denial; but at the same time it preserves the Jewish people from 'absolute treachery'. At the end of the text, there is an aphoristic line: 'The Jews must be witnesses of the impossible, whether they want to or not' (*Die Juden müssen für das Unmögliche zeugen, ob sie wollen oder nicht*). Once isolated, extracted from its determining context, this sentence can be read in two different ways, especially when one is aware of certain puns of Rosenzweig's:

1 The Jews must attest to (*zeugen*) the impossible, they are

witnesses of the impossible independently of their will.

2 The Jews must engender (*zeugen*) Jews, they must do so for and in the name of the impossible, even if they do not want to. A Jew who becomes a father *already* testifies – and without being able to oppose it – to the impossible. Jewish procreation and generation, is the impossible.

Let us return to the path.

A logic determines Rosenzweig's statements about the Jewish people, its essence and its existence, its essence such as it manifests itself in its existence, without mediation and thanks to the name which is silence. It is a logic of the immediate whose certitude resists or appears to resist the dialectic. Admittedly, there is a promise, a tradition, a law: however, it is as if the immediacy of the *Bezeugung* (of the name) forced the Jew to give up discourse. Can Rosenzweig then give a different *definition* of the way when it is a question of delimiting the way of Christianity, of assigning it a limit and stating its finitude? The Jew limits, delimits, but he never includes himself in the dialectic of exclusion and inclusion. On the contrary he includes it within himself, and if he finds himself affected by the scission of war it is rather by virtue of a sort of auto-limitation effected in the beyond: the Jew does not depend on a limit. He represents the truth of the limit on the limit which still separates him from truth, from the uttering of the sacred name in silence or *as* silence: this limit is other than any other limit. It makes the Jewish people the only people and is therefore not the limit that defines a singularity. Holy war belongs to the 'mythic past' of this people, Rosenzweig states. The Jew represents a truth the becoming of which does not bear the mark of necessity, of dialectical movement. Definition is and must be, by definition, an attestation (*Bezeugung*). The Jews participate in that from which they are *a priori* excluded. Their participation excludes the participation of others, since they draw the limits with the rigour of truth. This is why *we* refers both to Jews and to Christians by associating and separating them. Certainly, the Jew who 'turns his back to the exterior and turns inward to the interior' can become 'hard, proud or rigid', even though he 'cannot descend into his own interior without at the same time ascending to the Highest'.[24] And it is also true that the Jew who

tends to forget creation and the way must undergo the experience (*Er-leben*) of 'Jewishness' (*Jüdischkeit*). There is, therefore, a
Jewish way, a waiting which is also an initiation: the Jew must
free himself from what is proper to him at birth in order to
reach what will be proper to him at the moment of his death.[25]
(Ginevra Bompiani emphasises the initiatory character of a
certain waiting.[26]) But is it enough to emphasise these limits? Is
it enough to bring oneself back to this supplementary limitation
which seems to contradict what Rosenzweig says elsewhere, to
show that the eternal way is the simple and symmetrical
complement of eternal life? Asking the question does not imply
a denial of the fact that within the system a certain parallelism,
a 'chiasmus' (this is an expression of Stéphane Mosès's), characterises the relationship between Judaism and Christianity.

The double eternity: Christianity and Judaism

Rosenzweig's commentary concerns not only what Maimonides
says about divine ways, but also what he says about man's 'great
error': 'It introduces the subsequent sentences about the way of
the true Messiah and about the great error of worshipping
another besides God into which the world was led [...] And
our great teacher continues thus. All these matters only served
to clear the way for King Messiah.'[27] Men have fallen into
error, they have dared to worship another: this was able to
happen because divine ways are essentially different from
human ways. From the moment there is more than one way –
and this is the moment when we experience the way – we can
choose the wrong way, we have already chosen the way that
leads us away from truth, that brings us to misfortune. But
according to Maimonides, quoted and commented on by
Rosenzweig, straying from the path only 'smoothes the road
for the Messiah'. Passing through catastrophe and within a
hair's breadth of the worst to touch salvation appears to be
necessary: we cannot but choose this way, this other way which
offers itself to us, even if it is the wrong way. What else could
the experience of the way be? The experience of the way is, in
this context, the experience of the wrong way; turning away
from and returning to the right way, the path which will be the
path of the Messiah: 'But when the true King Messiah will

appear and succeed, be exalted and lifted up, they will forthwith recant (*kehren sie alle heim*) and realise that they have inherited naught but lies from their fathers.' Turning away is a misrecognition, returning a recognition of the path, of the way that leads to God.

But this straying, this parting from the way which is originally the Jews' aberration, must be distinguished from history as Christian history or as 'the way through time'. Christian experience is a passing through time which inscribes itself in eternity: the way travels through time without being divided by it. It establishes the divisions of time. The way is older and younger than time, the time that Rosenzweig defines as 'older and younger than everything that occurs'.[28] So the advent of Christianity must be considered as an event – as an event without equal and unlike anything which occurs in time. An event suspends time: this suspension which is a suspension of meaning can give rise to another interpretation of time. Before any interpretation, the event irrupts as the presentation of meaning as such. The advent of Christianity must be considered as an event, since the way confers a meaning or a signification upon time, more precisely: upon the present. Thinking Christianity, thinking the way, comes back to thinking time on the basis of this way; it thus comes back to thinking the epoch. For to master or measure time, Christianity must turn the present into an epoch: 'The epoch no longer passes before I am aware of it [...] If then the present too were to be elevated to the mastery of time, it too would have to be a between. The present – every present – would have to become "epoch-making".'[29] The way is what institutes an epoch; the past points to the way; time itself becomes subject to the way: 'Only the time before Christ's birth is now still past. All the time that succeeds, from Christ's earthly sojourn to his second coming, is now that sole great present, that epoch, that standstill, that suspension of the times, that interim over which time has lost its power. Time is now mere temporality (*bloße Zeitlichkeit*).'[30] Obviously we could link this to all Nietzsche says about the spirit of vengeance. Heidegger deals with it at length, as Jacques Derrida reminded us in his seminar. Time as sign of *unterwegs*, of being *on the way*,[31] is a time which is mastered. What do we do when we want to transform the present into an epoch and a sign so that we can master and comprehend time? When we immobilise or reify[32] flowing time by submitting it to the measure of the eternal way? What we do can be interpreted as the vengeance of the will which cannot abide the time of 'purely temporal vitality' (*rein zeitliche Lebendigkeit*) because it escapes it. In which case it is difficult to overlook the affinity between Christianity and Judaism, between eternal way and life. Is the detour of Christianity a return to Judaism? Rosenzweig specifies that it is not eternity but what is eternal that makes the difference. Time becomes the way, the one way, a way the beginning and end of which are necessarily beyond time; otherwise time could not become one-way. The way is eternal. It differentiates itself from the temporal way which leads from time to time. On the temporal way, 'only the next segment can ever be surveyed'.[33] On the eternal way, however, the distance which separates each point from the beginning and end is always the same. When one is on the temporal way, one does not see the way, one sees only a part of the way: the way becomes time. On the eternal way, one 'sees' nothing but the way, one 'sees' nothing, nothing else, one 'sees' only the beginning and the end: eternity. 'Thus the three periods of time have separated into eternal beginning, eternal middle and eternal end of the eternal path through this temporality.'[34] The one who walks on the eternal way knows that 'beginning and end are both equally near to him at every moment, for both are in the eternal, and it is only thereby that he knows himself as midpoint at every moment'.[35] The eternal way makes the event perpetual, it is the centre where the event takes place continuously. The event is the eternal way as perpetuity of the centre. Each singular event (*Ereignis*) is dependent on the event itself (*Geschehen*): 'Every event (*Ereignis*) stands midway between beginning and end of the eternal path and, by virtue of this central position in the temporal middle of eternity, every event is itself eternal.'[36] But is the man who 'sees' the beginning and the end, who 'sees' the way and the centre, at the centre of a 'horizon'[37] that his gaze takes in? Is he capable of seeing more than he saw before? On the temporal way, he saw only part of the horizon. However, on the eternal way, he is 'as midpoint of a stretch, consisting entirely of midpoints, in short all middle, all between, all path'. What of the temporality of the eternal way? If all is way, if the way is nothing other than a pure in-between, it is an opening: the horizon is never able to form, to constitute itself as such. In other words, the man who walks on the eternal way is not a subject. The eternal way has no subject. Only the subject assures the identity of his representation by representing to himself beforehand the 'horizon' of representation. Every time that Heidegger describes subjectivity, that he analyses the structure of what he calls subjectivity, he uses the phenomenological concept of the 'horizon', especially in the *Kantbuch* and in one of the lecture courses on Nietzsche. But we must not forget that the concept also appears when Heidegger sets out the temporal structure of *Dasein* and that it is one of the last three words of *Being and Time*. In his discussion of releasement, Heidegger writes: 'Releasement (*Gelassenheit*) is indeed the release of oneself from transcendental re-presentation and so a relinquishing of the willing of a horizon.' And: 'What is evident of the horizon, then, is but the side facing us of an openness which surrounds us (*eines uns umgebenden Offenen*); an openness which is filled with views (*Aussicht*) of the appearances (*Aussehen*) of what to our re-presenting are objects.'[38] I am not claiming that Rosenzweig, in challenging the concept of horizon (which he does not dwell on in *The Star* ...), has in mind the same thing that Heidegger understands by the *being-horizon of the horizon*. Nonetheless, the refusal of the term may indicate the necessity of distancing oneself from the subject of philosophy, representation and method. To say that the way has no subject is to imply that there is no method either, that the movement is not methodical. Here, method does not simply refer to what Heidegger defines, loosely, as 'the path upon which we pursue (*nachgehen*) a matter',[39] but to what he defines, more precisely and by referring to the properly modern sense of the word as 'the securing, conquering proceeding against beings, in order to capture them as objects for the subject' (*das sichernde, erobernde Vor-gehen gegen Seiendes, um es als Objekt sicherzustellen*).[40]

The eternity of the way and the eternity of life or blood are not identical. Consequently, it is the spirit, the holy water of baptism, which makes the way eternal. What does this spiritual character of the way lead us to think? Maybe this: spirit always has a relationship with the way and the path, mediation and translation, turning away and returning, the mission and the word. It dies because it speaks all languages, because it has a 'thousand languages (*Zungen*) in its mouth'. It wants everything to become its property. But by dying, it can resurrect:

> Christianity, as the eternal way, has to spread ever further. Merely to preserve its status would mean for it renouncing its eternity and therewith death. Christianity must proselytise. This is just as essential to it as self-preservation through shutting the pure spring of blood off from foreign admixture is to the eternal people. Indeed proselytising is the veritable form of its self-preservation for Christianity [...] In the eternal people, procreation (*Erzeugung*) bears witness (*Zeugnis*) to eternity; on the eternal way this witness must really be attested to as witness (*Zeugnis*) [...] There the physical onward flow of the one blood (*fleischliches Fortströmen des einen Bluts*) bears witness (*bezeugt*) to the ancestor in the engendered (*gezeugt*) grandson. Here the outpouring of the spirit (*Ausgiessung des Geistes*) must establish the communion of testimony (*Gemeinschaft des Zeugnisses*) in the uninterrupted stream of baptismal water coursing on from each to another.[43]

The spirit translates; language is the vital condition of the spiritual: 'It is the first effect of the spirit to translate, to erect a bridge between man and man, between tongue and tongue [...] And spirit means precisely that the translator, the one who hears and transmits, knows himself equal to the One who first spoke and received the word. Spirit thus leads man [...] It is man's own spirit precisely as the spirit of transmission and translation.'[42] The mission reveals itself to be essentially a spiritual transmission. Man's humanity, what is essential to him, announces itself on the basis of that which announces, on the basis of the announcement itself. The spirit of transmission announces Man. Men recognise each other thanks to the *Losungswort*, the rallying cry, the watchword,[43] the password which unites them, which shows that they belong to the community of the way. Spirit, language, the spiritual unity of the *Losungswort* whose function is that of a name allows the believer to 'attain to something' in the world. What he believes in is not, however, the object of thought in the same way that spirit, here, does not point to the subjective unity of thought or its identity. Where there is a *Losungswort*, we also find a way. The *Losungswort* traces the path of recognition. If the Christian community becomes unified through its attested faith and if the 'content' of that faith is the way, then the unity of the one way as the spiritual unity of a *Losungswort* must be recognised as the foundation of Christianity and as its very spirituality. The Christian knows that he believes, that he awaits the return − of Christ − and that his life is on the eternal way. That is his faith, the 'content' of his testimony: in its solitude, in the solitude of the singular soul, he testifies to his faith which is faith in some-thing. By testifying, by attesting his faith, by attesting to some-thing he engenders (*erzeugen*) the eternal way, in a spiritual engendering. At the other extreme, Jewish faith is 'the product of an engendering' (*Erzeugnis einer Zeugung*) which is not or not simply spiritual. It is not a form of knowledge and it has no content: 'the Jew, engendered a Jew (*der als Jude Gezeugte*), attests (*bezeugt*) his belief by continuing to procreate (*fortzeugen*) the Jewish people. His belief is not in something: he is himself the belief. He is believing with an immediacy that no Christian dogmatist can ever achieve for himself. This belief cares little for its dogmatic fixation: it has existence and that means more than words.'[44] An attestation that attests to pure existence and can do without language, existence that attests to itself, without words, in the act, attests to nothing: it is not spiritual enough. From the moment that Jewish attestation resists transmission and dogmatic translation it is no longer attestation − at least from a Christian point of view − for to translate means to attest, to testify. Testifying, Rosenzweig tells us, is always 'an indivi-dual matter' (*Sache des Einzelnen*), a matter for an individuality that remains inconceivable for the Jews, whose determination consists in engendering further generations of their people by blood. This is what drives the others, the Christians, mad. This madness of the spirit is perhaps an effect of the untranslatable, of what simultaneously commands and forbids translation:

And withal: the Jew does it [he accuses the 'faith which pursues its victorious way throughout the world' of being profoundly mythic, A.G.D.]. Not with words, for what would words still avail in this realm of vision! But with his existence, his silent existence. This existence of the Jew constantly subjects Christianity to the idea that it is not attaining the goal, the truth, that it ever remains – on the way. This is the profoundest reason for the Christian hatred of the Jew, which is heir to the pagan hatred of the Jew. In the final analysis it is only self-hate, directed to the objectionable mute admonisher, for all that he but admonishes by his existence; it is hatred of one's own imperfection, one's own not-yet [...] The Jew sanctified his flesh and blood under the yoke of the law and thereby lives constantly in the reality of the heavenly kingdom; the Christian's constantly profane flesh and blood sets itself in opposition to redemption, and he learns that he himself is not permitted to anticipate redemption emotionally. By anticipating redemption, the Jew purchases the possession of truth with the loss of the unredeemed world; he gives the lie to the Christian who, on his march of conquest into the unredeemed world, has to purchase his every forward step with illusion, with madness (*Wahn*).[45]

If the Jew is in a position to renounce discourse because he is the word itself and the name (this renunciation and the anticipation of redemption express the meaning of sanctification), then the Christian who dwells outside of the name and who therefore must walk on the eternal way becomes mad by attaching too much importance to the word, by misrecognising its value. The madness of the spirit reminds us of the living body of a silent existence, as if the spirit were waiting for this body without admitting it and turned against it because it revealed this wait, the wait which it interrupted, which it wanted to interrupt. As long as there is Christian hatred towards Judaism, Christianity will not have interrupted Jewish waiting and will remain a pagan religion. Is a pagan religion still or already a religion, doesn't it belong to what Rosenzweig calls 'myth'? But the 'myth' itself is double, it has a double unity, a unity and a double. It is the unity of the myth which carries the Jewish people beyond all contradiction, out of the world and history. The 'mythic past' of the Jews is inseparable from this power of the myth, from this unity which puts the future within the people's grasp:

> The Jew alone suffers no conflict between the supreme vision which is placed before his soul and the people among whom his life has placed him. He alone possesses the unity of *the* myth which the nations lost through the influx of Christianity, which they were bound to lose, for their own myth was pagan myth which, by leading them into itself, led them away from God and their neighbour. The Jew's myth, leading him into his people, brings him face to face with God who is also the God of all nations. The Jewish people feels no conflict between what is its very own and what is supreme; the love it has for itself inevitably becomes love for its neighbour.[46]

As we have seen, hatred only reinforces the will to wait, provided we can speak, in this context, of a 'will'. But if it is true that hatred reinforces the will to wait, as sentences of the type 'the Jew gives the lie to the Christian' suggest to us, it is because it runs up against a will; against a will to exist (*Wille zum Volk*, 'will to be a people').[47] All Christians are missionaries. Each time a Christian missionary succeeds, the Jewish people takes root even more deeply in itself. Existence escapes the spirit insofar as the spirit affirms its power through its discourse. Every mission is transmission; every mission is thus impossible since it is affected by the fatal logic of the untranslatable.[48]

Silence and gesture

The immediacy of Jewish experience is the immediacy of a silence (*Schweigen*), of a silent existence which, through its very silence, comes close to the name as silence. What does it mean to experience silence as the essence of language and as the completely condensed word (*das ganz gesammelte Wort*)? The silence experienced is 'unlike the muteness (*Stummheit*) of the protocosmos (*Vorwelt*), which had no words yet'. It is 'a silence which no longer has any need of the word.'[49] Being silent is not the same as being mute, and if we were forced to decide, we would have to acknowledge that it is actually Christianity which is – still – mute. It is mute because of its eloquence. The experience of silence is language: language, the 'diversity of languages' marks the path which leads from proto-cosmic or pre-worldly mutism to trans-worldly silence. This privilege granted to silence, this dignity of silence which 'no longer has any need of the word', which is more essential than the word, which is the word as such (is it possible to speak of a mystical thought here?), may also be found in *Being and Time* when Heidegger writes that the call which calls *Dasein* to appear before its own potentiality for being itself 'does not put itself into words at all: yet it remains nothing less than obscure and indefinite'.[50] The silence which Rosenzweig speaks of is 'the silence of completed understanding'. Let me point out in passing that this sentence could be compared not only with certain paragraphs of *Being and Time* but also with a text of Benjamin's entitled 'The Metaphysics of Youth'.[51] Where silence lets itself be understood as the silence of completed understanding, 'one glance says everything'. This passage from language to the glance is a true passage, not a 'miserable surrogate for communication'. The glance which says everything says more than can be said. All at once or in the blink of an eye, the glance exceeds language:

> Nothing shows so clearly that the world is unredeemed as the diversity of languages. Between men who speak a common language, a glance would suffice for reaching an understanding; just because they speak a common language, they are elevated above speech. [Thus we never speak a common language: the *Losungswort* is beyond language, it is the opening of language, A.G.D.] Between different languages, however, only the stammering word mediates, and the gesture ceases to be immediately intelligible as it had been in the mute glance of the eye (*im stummen Blick des Auges*). It is reduced to a halting sign language, that miserable surrogate for communication. [The *Losungswort* is inevitable for Christianity because it represents the experience of the difference between languages; Judaism does not need such a word, at least to the extent that it is already, and this by virtue of its very existence, the silence of completed understanding, A.G.D.] As a result the supreme component in

liturgy is not the common word but the common gesture. Liturgy frees gesture from the fetters of helpless servitude to speech, and makes of it Something more than speech.[52]

This long quote comes from the introduction that precedes the three books that form the third part of *The Star* ... It is important to note that gesture does not imitate language: it is not a rudimentary or primitive form of language, nor another language. Gesture is the other which constitutes language because comprehension depends on the sharing of language. In the second book, in the chapter on the eternal way, Rosenzweig insists on the relevance of the gesture – but it must not be forgotten that kneeling plays a decisive part in Jewish religion, given that Judaism can only anticipate the redemption. The simplest gesture is the glance:

> The power to dissolve all that is rigid already inheres in the glance. It is a power which remained unattainable to the deed (*Tat*), a power for whose sake the word sacrificed itself if only to master it at this cost for the brief pause before the answer. A word forgets itself and is to be forgotten; it wants to perish in the answer. The power of the glance, however, does not perish with the moment. Once an eye has glanced at us, it will glance at us as long as we live.[53]

The gesture is not a deed. Its potency, the strength with which it resists disappearance, time and forgetting, comes from the difference which separates it from both language and the deed. And yet, all language comprises a gesture or a sign. The sign, excessive and singular, always remains unanswered, and we do nothing other than respond to it, we do nothing but attempt to respond to language, to the gesture or the sign which it necessarily comprises and which is not reducible to it. We do not respond to some linguistic proposition or other, we seek the gesture. A response, a word encountering another word, is also a word, something other than a word, in search of the word of the *other*, the other of the word. Consequently, what cannot be erased in a response, the glance, watches us, keeps us our whole life, even if we have forgotten it.[54] It is the glance of the other which does not forget. But the gesture or sign remains unseen as long as we do not approach the name and its silence. Thus it is not we who keep and hold names, but names that keep and watch us. We can keep names because they already keep us, and they keep us because something in them, something related to the gesture or sign, draws us towards silence. At the edge of the path, of the way, of language, we experience something very simple: something, maybe a name, maybe the other of the name, the name as other, watches us in the silence.[55]

That which watches and concerns us

What watches us? What keeps us by watching us? I draw on Rosenzweig to suggest this hypothesis: nothing could watch us if we were only waiting for death. For death keeps nothing, it is the absolute event, it doesn't even watch us. The alterity of the name, the gesture or the sign is not the alterity of death. It is the alterity of the future. Of course, death inscribes itself in the future, but the future would not be a future if it let itself be determined by the certainty of the indeterminable, of death. Death watches us so much that the gaze becomes blind: we recognise death by seeing another who is dead or dying, but this recognition does not imply any knowledge, it blinds us. The gaze of the name watches us and keeps us because it is the condition of possibility of the relation to the other, of this relationship which is interrupted by death and marked beforehand by this very interruption. The names say: 'At least help me so that death comes to us only from us. Do not give in to generality.'[56] Like the recognition of death, the recognition of the gesture or the sign does not presuppose any previous knowledge. But if it blinds us it is because it puts us in relation with a future of which we know nothing. Death has no future, which is not to say that the future is death. And yet: can't the dead return, can't they keep a surprise in store for us?[57] And what if the alterity of death and the alterity of the future were not absolutely incompatible? And what if this were alterity, death other than the future, the future other than death, the death and the future of the other?[58] 'That which has a name of its own', Rosenzweig writes, 'can no longer be a thing, no longer everyman's affair. It is incapable of utter absorption into the category for there can be no category for it to belong to; it is its own category.'[59]

The gift of the name is the other of the death which the name carries within itself. However, Rosenzweig does not speak of this reaching beyond, which situates the name beyond the life of the one who is named:

> For only Others can die; Man dies only as an Other, as a He. The I cannot conceive of itself as dead. Its fear of death is the horror of becoming the only thing that its eyes can see in the deceased Others: a deceased He, a deceased It [...] As often as he sees a dead man, a breath of fear blows over the living, and this breath comes over the living man whenever he conceives of himself as a dead man, for strictly speaking one can never conceive of 'oneself' as a dead man, but only of 'Another'. Oneself thus out-lives the other, every other, regardless. For the other, every other, is dead simply by being another, from eternity on. He was created as another, and as created being he becomes completed creature in death; as created being he is not destined, in the final analysis, to out-live (*über-leben*) any other. For life is not the apex of creation. Its destiny is to out-die itself (*sich zu übersterben*). Not life but death perfects the created thing into an individual solitary thing. Death endows it with the supreme solitude of which, as thing among things, it is capable.[60]

Only others can die, I die as the other, I am other when I die, the other dies; but only the other, other in relation to the thing, keeps the future by signalling to us. Thus we are watched from the end of the path, that is to say, from the limits of language, where the detour and the return can no longer be told apart, where the detour can become a return.

An open question: is the glance mostly Christian, mostly pagan? Or is it also Jewish? Must we reach something that the glance cannot? Is this thing mostly Jewish? Or is it also Christian? It is Christian because it was previously Jewish? 'The mouth is consummator and fulfiller of all expression of which the countenance is capable, both in speech as, at last, in the silence behind which speech retreats: in the kiss. It is in the eyes that the eternal countenance shines for man; it is the mouth by whose words man lives. But for our teacher Moses, who in his lifetime was privileged only to see the land of his desire (*Sehn-sucht*), not to enter into it, God sealed this completed life with a kiss of his mouth. Thus does God seal and so too does man.'[61] This passage must be read in conjunction with another passage:

> Wherever it [that which has a name of its own] is, there is a midpoint, and wherever it opens its mouth, there is a begin-ning [...] There must be a where in the world, a still visible spot whence revelation radiates, and a when, a yet echoing moment, where revelation first opened its mouth. Both must have been one and the same at one time, though no longer today, something as united in itself as my experi-ence is today. For it is supposed to put my experience (*Erleb-nis*) on a firm foundation [...] The ground of the revelation is midpoint and beginning in one; it is the revela-tion of the divine name [...] For name is in truth word and fire, and not sound and fury (*Schall und Rauch*) as unbe-lief would have it again and again in obstinate vacuity. It is incumbent to name the name and to acknowledge: I believe it.[62]

(For Rosenzweig, the question of the proper name is related to the question of the solitude of the Self who has no mouth – here we must re-read the *Metaethics*.[63] The man with a proper name is the only one who can open his mouth and reply to the divine call. See the second part of the second book of *The Star* ...) Is the eternal way the distance between eyes and mouth? Is God's seal at the same time the origin and the end of eternal life? What is it to seal? Is it to reveal the name at the moment when language passes into silence?

II

Of the path-like nature of thought

One might be tempted to say that Heidegger never thought the path as a temporal or an eternal path, as a method, or as a meta-physical or an onto-theological concept. Isn't the thought of the path, as it becomes decisive for Heidegger, what leads us to the borders of subjectivity, far away from it? If we ask the question overhastily in these terms, we risk not taking a certain way of thinking, which does not seem to lead in this direction, into account. For example, here is a quote from his 'Rectoral Address': 'Only a spiritual world gives the people the assurance of greatness. For it necessitates that the constant decision between the will to greatness and a letting things happen that means decline, will be the law presiding over the march that our people has begun into its future history.'[64] In this passage there is a relationship between the question of thought – it is the spiritual world which gives a people its greatness, Jacques Derrida has stressed this aspect of spirit[65] – and the question of the path – the German people, this people which engenders its own spiritual world, is on the march: it advances along the path of spirit according to the law of a *Schrittgesetz*, step by step. The relation between the two questions is very obvious: the question of the path, of the path of a *Marsch*, is linked to a will (*Wille zur Größe*) which would be difficult to distinguish from subjectivity. However, I think that it would oversimplify things to claim that Heidegger once, in a certain epoch, strayed from the right path, the proper path. Why? Perhaps because by saying so we would be forced to speak in the name of a thought of the path the entire point of which consists, precisely, in showing the essential character of straying: there is no right path. We can ask ourselves, of course, if *Vorstellung*, representation, is really a form of *Verstellung*, if it blocks the path which leads to the essence of the path, and if we must suppose a certain uncontaminated origin, a certain purity, a certain rightness of the path. Jacques Derrida raised this question in a text on the *Discourse on Method*.[66] Does Heidegger allow straying from the path to be thought differently, as something other than straying between path and method, between two paths which do not differ from themselves?

'In fact the path bears his name: Martin-Heidegger-Weg', writes Philippe Lacoue-Labarthe at the beginning of a text remembering a date and included in his book *La poésie comme expérience*.[67] He first describes a visit to Todtnauberg; then he names a text of Heidegger's which he translated with Roger Munier: 'The Want of Sacred Names'. He then emphasises the fact that in a poem and lecture by Celan, 'not just poetry (every

poem) but the very thought of poetry itself appears as "path".'
He adds that 'Celan could not have not been thinking of
Heidegger'. I would like to ask myself in turn, following this
trace, what becomes of the path in Heidegger, the path of the
poem and the path named by a poem. The text 'The Want of
Sacred Names', which deals with the path-like character of
thought, gathers together all the relevant motifs; it deals with
Denken (thought), *Dichten* (poetry, but not just in the sense of
lyric poems), *Seinsvergessenheit* (the forgetting of Being), *Not*
(peril, need, distress, necessity), *Geschick* (destiny, sending), *Lich-
tung* (the clearing of Being as *aletheia*), *Gestellnis* (not *Gestell*, the
framework of technology) and the *offene Gegend* (open region).
What may be surprising is the fact that all these motifs, all these
Losungsworte of Heidegger's thought, intersect in the question of
the 'want of sacred' or holy 'names'. Why is it that Heidegger
names the name, the sacred name named by Hölderlin, at the
moment when he seems to be gathering everything together,
almost everything that he has thought in thirty years? I will
now quote the end of his text. Two words must be noted;
Heidegger speaks of a blinding and of a gaze:

> Yet as long as the gaze of the path (*Wegblick*) remains denied
> to us, and as long as we don't see that even in the withdra-
> wal and self-reserve of presencing, presencing rules in its
> own way (*Anwesen*), so long we shall remain blind toward
> and unmoved by the oppressive coming-into-presence which
> belongs to the want of sacred or holy names, a want which
> shelters the name of the holy and the holy itself and nonethe-
> less conceals (*verbirgt*) it. Only a sojourn in the open Region
> out of which the want of holy names presences holds (*birgt*)
> the possibility of an insight (*Einblick*) into that which today *is*
> inasmuch as it is wanting.[68]

The whirl: Wege *and* Winke

'*Wege*'[69] is the title of a poem Heidegger wrote in 1970 – four
years before he wrote 'The Want of Sacred Names' – and
which is part of the collection called *Gedachtes*. It is hardly
surprising that Heidegger chose the name *Gedachtes* and not
Gedichtetes: the more a poet is what he is, the more he is a

thinker, the more he is other than what he is, the more he exposes himself to what he is not. Heidegger says as much in a letter to Emil Staiger in 1950 (*ein Dichter ist freilich um so dichtender, je denkender er ist*).[70] It is thus a case of poetry, *Dichtung*, being exposed to thought, *Denken* – I am using here the terms found in another of Heidegger's letters: this time sent to Max Kommerell in 1942.[71] Poetry is its own exposure to thought. Thought is proper to poetry. Here is a thinker who cannot expose himself to thought except by becoming that which he is not, a poet. It will have been necessary for him to expose himself to poetry in order to expose himself to thought, to think exposed thought, thought itself. When thought exposes itself, something arrives, perhaps poetry. I will limit myself to quoting and discussing the first line of '*Wege*': *Wege, Wege des Denkens, gehende selber, entrinnende* ('Paths, paths of thought, going by themselves, vanishing'). Paths, paths of thought go by themselves, they follow a path: is this path a sort of meta-path? This is unlikely, as such a doubling-up would be meaningless. If there is a path that guarantees the path to take, why then speak of a path which follows another path, which finds itself on the way, which itself walks whilst vanishing? We must go further. Is this other path which is not a meta-path still a path? Doesn't vanishing (*entrinnen*) mark the withdrawal of the path into the path? The path doubles up, but there is no other path to follow, there is no path of the path, there is no representation of the path. The path is not the path of a story, or a teleology, or a subject. If we know in advance, through taking the path in with a glance, that it has a unity and that it leads us to an exact place, the path is no longer a path. It is only a path if it strays from itself: it is its own straying, a straying that cannot become a property of the path. The path strays. Anyone who tries to pin it down is caught in a vertiginous whirl, in a whirl where paths do not intersect but where the path opens onto the opening, onto the void of its origin. It is perhaps this irreducible straying which allows method to inscribe itself along the path; at the same time, however, straying ruins all method. The path never stops straying and vanishing. One does not follow a path, one finds oneself on it without knowing where one is going: the path is going, it has already left. But the path is neither a moving walkway nor a path which itself knows where it is going or which, in leaving, appropriates to itself all the stages of its turns and detours. Also, finding oneself on a path without knowing where one is going does not in the least mean that one is going nowhere in particular and doing nothing in particular. It means that there is not *one* path, that there are only stretches of path, and that another bit of path can cross the one on which one finds oneself. The poem that Heidegger gives us to read after '*Wege*' is '*Winke*', which we translate poorly as 'Signs' or 'Hints', but how else can we translate the word *Wink*? In *On the Way to Language*, Heidegger distinguishes between *Winke* and *Gebärden*, hints and gestures, and *Zeichen* and *Chiffren*, signs and ciphers.[72] The sign (*Zeichen*) is supposed to belong to the metaphysics that the hint (*Wink*) exceeds. Can we notice hints other than in passing? 'Hints need the widest sphere in which to swing',[74] Heidegger notes. A certain indeterminacy is essential to the *Wink*. Is the gesture to which our attention is drawn and which distracts us really a *Wink*? The *Wink* has no presence, it is always part of a past or of a future which cannot be (re)presented. A *Wink* seems to be intended for us. Our destiny and determination are tied to the *Wink* because it reminds us that we share the place we inhabit, that is, we share language. To notice a *Wink* is to experience alterity. Heidegger would say: to experience the divine. For to be divine means to signal: *Die Götter winken, indem sie sind* ('The gods signal by virtue of their existence').[74] The *Wink* is the origin of language, of the word; it is, according to the expression used in *On the Way to Language*, its essential or fundamental trait (*Grundzug des Wortes*). Isn't experiencing the alterity of language naming? Isn't naming noticing a *Wink* which is lost to identification and knowledge and without which there would be no language?

> To name is to unveil, to unconceal. It is a showing which allows something to be experienced. However, if such a showing must distance itself from the proximity of what is to be said, then the saying of the distant, being a saying-from-afar, becomes a calling. To the extent that that which is to be called is too close, it must be kept at a distance, it must be kept as something distant, it must remain 'obscure' under its very name. The name must veil it. Naming is a calling which unconceals, but as such it is also a call which conceals.[75]

The name signals, it calls and shows something: something, what must be named, called, what the name calls by disclosing and concealing it, what in the name as name is disclosed and concealed, what signals, calls the name as if the name were calling itself, but without closing in on itself. In naming, the name keeps the *Wink*, it watches itself, it is concerned with itself; this relation to itself, this relation of language to language is a relation of distancing, of disclosure which conceals and of concealment which discloses. The *Wink*, the fundamental characteristic of language, of the word, is nothing, certainly not an attribute or a function of language, of the name. It is equally not a *Losungswort*. Perhaps the *Wink* is just an opening which does not allow itself to be grasped as such, perhaps it is nothing but the alterity of language. Its relation to itself, which we experience when we name, is a vertiginous whirl. It is thus, in experiencing the name, the name yet to come, the shared and divided name, that we find ourselves on a path which is going by itself: *Wege, gehende selber*. And what if the poem, the *Gedicht*, were nothing other than a vertiginous whirl, a *Wirbel*? Could Heidegger not have written a poem, this poem? (We do not *know* that the poem is a whirl: we must experience the poem, enter into its movement, we must begin to walk; 'the first thing will be to start going'.)

> The poem is no longer a smooth text, possessing a straight 'meaning', quite the contrary, this linguistic configuration is in itself a whirl which carries us along somewhere. And not progressively, for it tears us away with hard brusqueness from the very beginning [...] But where does this whirl carry us? To the word of which the poem constitutes the linguistic configuration (*Sprachgefüge*). What is this word? Who speaks to whom, with whom, and about what? We are carried into a dialogue (*Gespräch*) which brings word to word, language to language, not as something arbitrary and anecdotal but as the mission entrusted to the young girl, to *Germania*: '*O, thou, daughter of the sacred land! Name* ... '; more precisely, it is a question of naming and saying.[76]

Is the *Wink* German, does it point towards Germany, towards

Germanien? The *Wink*, the address which gives us language, which makes us speak and name, is (at) the very origin of history, of all historical missions. The dialogue (which is also silence [*Schweigen*]) does not begin where 'historical' progress is already underway: the advent of the dialogue is the beginning of history. But, for Heidegger, it is the German people who must assume (*Sendung, Bestimmung, Auftrag*) history by assuming its language.

On the path towards sacred names: the experience of the name as the experience of a *Wink* or *Gebärde* is always the experience of a detour and a return, of the past and the future, of a memory and a promise. There is no return without a detour, and it is a question of a return when a *Wink* or a *Gebärde*, a hint or a gesture, make themselves noticed; for how could we notice them if we do not recognise them (we recognise them without recognising them)? Heidegger keeps one sentence to say the end, for the moment of awakening: 'What we said about the sleeping of Being means to say that being *as such* has not yet awakened so that It looks upon us from out of its awakened essence.'[77]

II

Translating the thing

In his essay 'The *Retrait* of Metaphor' Jacques Derrida speaks of a 'performance' or a 'performative of writing by which Heidegger names, calls *Aufriß* (incision) what he decides or decrees to call *Aufriß*, what he allows to come to be called *Aufriß* or what, according to him is called and calls itself *Aufriß*'. Derrida sketches the translation of this word following 'the traction of an equally performing gesture, by *incision*'. At stake is Heidegger's 'trenchant decision to call *Aufriß* what was in a certain way still unnamed or unknown under its name'. This decision, Derrida claims, 'is already in itself an incision; it can only be named, name itself, and be incised in its own writing'. He adds: 'There is a gesture here, or rather a gesture is *given* here which cannot be described as the gesture of producing a neologism or a meta-writing.'[78] What about the decision Derrida calls 'trenchant' in this difficult passage dealing with denomination and translation? What about the 'performative of writing' if what is still 'unnamed' is not really 'unnamed' but only 'unknown under its name', that is to say, if the 'performance' only states: this name is the name of the thing? What about denomination if it is a translation in a loose sense of the term, if it only makes clear what is already obvious 'in a certain way', even if the thing cannot yet appear? What about translation if it is a kind of denomination where there is not yet a language, a word or a name to translate?

It is precisely when developing his thoughts about naming that Benjamin gives some hints about the relevance of translating. For him it is necessary to root the concept of translation in the deepest layer of language. Therefore, thinking translation signifies thinking the name, since denomination is the source of language; it is language as the origin of human language. From the very beginning, there is translation. One cannot think translation after the fact; one cannot add the concept of translation to a 'linguistic theory' as if it were a merely secondary concept: 'It is necessary to found the concept of translation at the deepest level of linguistic theory, for it is much too far-reaching and powerful to be treated in any way as an afterthought, as has happened occasionally.'[79] There would be no language and thus no origin without translation. To think translation, we must think translation as denomination and denomination as translation. In Benjamin's text it is a question of a 'task' (*Aufgabe*) which God assigns to man: man must name things. He becomes what he is, he attains his humanity and communicates his spiritual essence through naming the things created by God. But denomination depends on how things communicate themselves to man: 'rather, the name which man gives to the thing (*Sache*) depends on how it communicates itself to him.'[80] The gift of giving names has been given to man: however, man cannot give names, he has no gift if nothing communicates, if he does not receive the gift of understanding the language of things. The 'gift of language' (*Gabe der Sprache*) is the gift of understanding this other language. Since the gift of language is the gift of denomination, since the gift is a task, since what is given to man is not a given and since the task of giving a name is inseparable from things letting-themselves-be-understood or giving-themselves-to-be-understood, the man who names is always a man who responds. As such he is a responsible man. Man assumes the responsibility of the task which God has given him when he responds to what he hears and when he receives what he understands as a gift. The responsible man assumes his freedom: can one conceive of a task without coneiving of freedom?[81] To give, man must have already received a gift, which does not mean to say that he contents himself with giving back this gift, for what meaning can be given to the human task if denomination is nothing more than the giving back or the reappropriation of the gift? Maybe it is inevitable that God reappropriates the gift to himself each time that man gives names to things. Maybe it is inescapable that man appropriates his essence through returning the gift; but for the gift to be a gift, those who give must not know what they are giving or doing. They must expose themselves in giving. This exposure is not opposed to man's task, on the contrary: if the gift did not involve exposure, man would have no task; he would only have technical knowledge.

Receiving the gift, conceiving the nameless (*empfangen*, not *entwerfen*), naming the thing: conception (*Empfängnis*) and spontaneity tie themselves together in human language. Benjamin claims that there is a word to designate this double structure of denomination, the originary and original structure of language. 'For conception (*Empfängnis*) and spontaneity together, which are found in this unique union only in the linguistic realm, language has its own word.'[82] This word, the word 'translation', is not only the right word, the word that suits the thing and the one that we choose from amongst all other words because it translates what the thing communicates better than the others. 'Translation' is the name that language has always had to call itself. The 'gift of language' is the gift of translation, of the word 'translation'; the task of man is the 'task of the translator'. Benjamin uses the expression *Empfängnis des Namenlosen im Namen* ('the conception of the nameless in the name') at the moment when he describes the singular liaison between *Empfängnis* and *Spontaneität*. This expression can be understood in two ways. (1) The nameless (Benjamin does not say *das Namenlose* but *das Unbenannte*, the unnamed, as the thing has been named by God) is in some way anterior to the name. However, it does not precede it. It passes through the name to be what it is. The name welcomes, engenders, allows that which has no name to appear. The name is the entry-way for the thing and its site. Man must name what is nameless. (2) Since it allows the nameless to appear, the name cannot be a name without being what it is not, what does not appear without it. The name must erase itself. That is why denomination is always over-naming. What is over-naming if it is not the erasing of the name? To name is to experience what is nameless, and this experience, according to Benjamin, is called translation.

Things have no names, they are nameless, *namenlos*, but there is a language of things. As things, that is as mute things, they speak to man. Human language is the translation of the language of things and to translate this language, man must name. Denomination implies a relation of affinity between the thing and the name: an affinity between two languages. It becomes possible and even necessary because language is not the other of the thing. If the mutism of the thing were absolute, if it were not the sign or the manifestation of another language, a magical language, the question of translation would never arise. As soon as we are dealing with another language, we are dealing with a demand for translation. This demand is all the more urgent since the language of things cannot be compared with just any language amongst the human languages. With regard to the language of names, human languages are mere derivations, deviations or degradations. The name receives the thing. We are reminded of the passage in 'The Metaphysics of Youth' where Benjamin compares the name with a jug brought towards meaning to receive it. The language of names is superior to the language it translates. However, the name that translates the thing can never translate another name. Isn't the fact that it is impossible to translate a name, a name in the sense of a proper, singular, unique name, the sign of the first translation that seems to command all translations? Doesn't it show the difference between the name and what is nameless and demands a translation? In 'The Task of the Translator', Benjamin claims that a translation which absorbs the content of the original and bears virtually no trace of its meaning, thus establishing a perfect harmony between languages, remains untranslatable. We understand now why he is so insistent on the fact that we cannot think translation without thinking language itself, its being, its essence. Translation must be translation of the other, of a language which is other, because there is more than one language: 'to identify naming language with language as such is to rob linguistic theory of its deepest insights.'[83]

The language of things and the language of names refer to divine language, the 'linguistic being' of God: 'For God created things; the creative word in them is the germ of the cognising name.' God assures the 'objectivity' of the original translation. What does this 'objectivity' consist of? The name does not content itself with receiving the thing and giving it a voice: to name is to add knowledge (*Erkenntnis*) to what is without knowledge, does not know itself, does not know the other. Through the name the thing becomes something recognised and known; a translation cannot do other than make the unknown knowable. One might think that translation adds a foreign element to language; in reality, it does nothing of the sort: translation closes the circle that the 'gift of language' opens by dissociating name and thing. It is a knowledge that recognises the thing, allows the thing to refer to itself through the name. The name is the self-reference of the thing in the sphere of knowledge. The thing translates itself into a name in order to appear as what it is. If the passage from the language of things into the language of names were barred, if no knowledge were possible, the translator would have no task. He would be confronted with a problem (*Aufgabe*) which has no solution. We couldn't even say that his *Aufgabe* is an *Aufgeben* in the sense of a necessary abandoning – Paul de Man draws our attention to this ambiguity in his paper on *The Task of the Translator*.[84] The language of things and the language of names belong to divine language, to the language of identity: in God name and word, knowledge and creation are identical. The language of things is the language of the word without name; inversely, the language of names is the language of the name without word.

What is a thing? Benjamin speaks of a 'magical community' of things which reveals itself to intuition (*Anschauung*) and is recognised by the name. Could we say, modifying Kant's line, that intuition without denomination would be blind? The idea of a 'magical community' seems very close to that of a nature or cosmos determined by a set of 'correspondences'; we find this idea in Benjamin, notably in the texts on the *mimetic faculty* and in the analyses that deal with Baudelaire. If the thing is already caught up in a network of 'correspondences' we never experience a thing without experiencing another thing, something else. So 'correspondences' – 'natural correspondences'[85] – create a 'community': a 'community' without name, without knowledge, without voice. It can be named, because a certain language is proper to it, because it is essential for the thing to communicate its 'spiritual content' to man: 'There is no event or thing in either animate or inanimate nature that does not in some way partake of language, for it is in the nature of all to communicate their spiritual content.'[86] Thinking the thing which is supposed to have a '*spiritual content*' on the basis of language and thus on the basis of translation means thinking 'communicability' and 'divisibility' (*Mit-teilbarkeit*) as decisive features of spirit. It is meaningless to imagine a being without language, a being which does not communicate its 'spiritual content': 'An existence entirely without relationship to language is an idea; but this idea can bear no fruit even within that realm of Ideas whose circumference defines the idea of God.'[87] To the extent that the thing must communicate, that communication belongs to it, its 'spiritual essence' is a 'linguistic essence'. Translation is the effect of the 'linguistic *essence*' of the thing and, consequently, of its spiritual character. In other words: the spirit of the thing – that which makes all experience possible and which is nothing but 'communicability' itself – commands its translation. But language is not simply the expression of some 'content', of a 'content' exterior to communication or enunciation: it is rather the expression of what is never said. That which is never said is 'saying' as the 'condition of possibility' of the 'said'. By 'spiritual content' we must understand the spiritual character of language, not a language of the spirit: 'What does language communicate? It communicates the spiritual essence corresponding to it. It is fundamental that this spiritual essence communicates itself *in* language and not *through* language.'[88] Benjamin gives an example reminiscent of an important motif of Heidegger's thought: German 'is by no means the expression of everything we could – theoretically – express *through* it, but is the immediate [*unmittelbar*: how is this immediacy to be understood? A.G.D.] expression of that which communicates *itself* in it.'[89] Translation is not the translation of what man says using language as a means of communication which has no relation to the thing: from the moment language becomes a means of communication and does not communicate itself, it strays away from itself. Translation translates language as language, that is to say, as the expression of the spirit which expresses only expression. Since language is not the representation of a 'speaking subject' (*Sprecher der Sprache*) translation represents nothing. In translation or as translation, language marks itself. For language does nothing other than mark itself: 'There is no such thing as a content of language.'[90] A 'linguistic essence' without the spirit is inconceivable; equally we cannot conceive of a 'spiritual essence' without language.

However, the 'spiritual essence' and the 'linguistic essence' do not seem to coincide: 'The distinction between a spiritual essence and the linguistic essence in which it communicates is the most originary distinction of any study of linguistic theory.'[91] We need to understand the necessity of this distinction which Benjamin does not hesitate to call 'the most originary'. It arises at the origin, it comes from the origin. The purest expression (*das Ausgesprochenste*) is also the most spiritual expression. Language is the 'immediacy' (*Unmittelbarkeit*) of spiritual communication; we must not confuse a language with a means of communication which remains indifferent towards a determined content. The 'immediacy' that Benjamin speaks of escapes from calculation and from any regulatory principle which would dominate language from outside. It is as if language never ceased to turn around itself and return to itself so as to stop any 'content' that could not return to it from appearing. The language of the thing is 'magical' because it stands in its own immanence, because the lack of content devotes it to its own 'immediacy'. Thinking that translation assures the mastery of a means of communication when it is lacking is a misrecognition of the 'magic of language'. A translation is by definition a 'transformation' of language or, more precisely, a multiplicity of uninterrupted transformations: 'Translation is a passage from one language into another through a continuum of transformations.'[92] But it is not enough to say that translation is a transformation: we must say that we cannot translate a superior language. We cannot do other than translate an inferior language, transform an inferior language into a superior one. Compared with the language that must be translated, the language that translates is always superior: 'every evolved language (with the exception of the word of God) can be considered as a translation of all others.' A language's superiority can be deduced from the fact that translation, this movement of faithfulness to language, must necessarily surpass the language to be translated in order to show the affinity between languages and so reach their essence, 'communicability'. This proposition already implies the answers to the following questions. Why is translation necessary? What does the transformation consist of if translation marks only itself, that is, if it only shows 'communicability'? What is the difference between one language and another? The differences between languages are those of media that are distinguished as it were by their density, that is, gradually; and this with regard to the density both of the communicating and of the communicable aspects of communication.'[93] Different languages have different characteristic densities. This density depends on the one hand on what communicates or gives something to understand to someone, and on the other on what has been communicated. The thing communicates without knowing what it communicates; hearing the thing is to hear a language without name and without voice. Conversely, hearing the man who names is to hear the language of names and know the thing. The name is the essence of language: there is no language more dense, intense and extensive than the language of names. The language of names is the translation of *all* other languages. Each time it is named, the name calls. It invokes and evokes language because it is its name. To name the name is to call upon man to achieve translation and allow the name to appear as *das innerste Wesen der Sprache selbst*. The proclamation and exclamation of the name indicate translation is nearing its end:

> The name, however, is not only the last utterance (*Ausruf*) of language but also the true call (*Anruf*) of it. Thus in the name appears the essential law of language, according to which to express (*aussprechen*) oneself and to address (*ansprechen*) everything else amounts to the same. Language – and in it a spiritual essence – only expresses (*aussprechen*) itself purely where it speaks in [the] name, that is, in its universal naming. So in the name culminate both the intensive totality of language, as the absolutely communicable spiritual essence, and the extensive totality of language, as the universally communicating (naming) essence. By virtue of its communicating nature, its universality, language is incomplete where the spiritual essence that speaks from it (*aus ihr spricht*) is not in its whole structure linguistic, that is, communicable. *Man alone has a language that is complete both in its universality and in its intensiveness.*[94]

Is the difference between languages the same as the difference between language and spirit? Benjamin does not seem very clear on this point: he claims that only man's spiritual essence can give itself to be understood without remainder, absolutely; he then says that the spiritual essence and the linguistic essence of things are in harmony. Saying that the linguistic essence of a thing is spiritual only in so far as its spirit gives itself to be understood would be to advance a tautological argument. The spiritual essence is nothing other than the linguistic essence; however, there is a difference between the spiritual essence and the language of the thing: a difference or a distinction which is 'the most originary' of all differences and distinctions, at once imperceptible and decisive. If the spiritual essence is communicability itself, it may designate nothing, nothing we can identify; it designates what makes communicability what it is and makes it communicate itself as communicability; it designates the incommunicable and untranslatable at the heart of communicability, of language, of the name. The incommunicable is not the negation of communicability, it does not oppose itself to language, it is not in conflict with communication and communicability ('the conflict between the expressed and expressible on one hand and the inexpressible and unexpressed on the other'), it is not the concept Benjamin rejects. The incommunicable does not hide any content, it has no meaning: it *is* communicability.

But can we conceive of a language without content, a language that has only its own essence as content, 'communicability'? How can we experience a language which gives itself to itself? Must we not, to start with, think the difference between languages as a difference inscribed in content? In his writings on resemblance and the 'mimetic faculty', Benjamin speaks of the 'semiotic'. The 'semiotic' designates the 'meaning' of the thing, what it means to say: to refer to the 'semiotic' is to refer to language as an intermediate term in communication. But if we stick to the logic of the text on language in general, we must define the 'semiotic' as the expression of a density which can never correspond to the density of the language of names. 'Meaning' in the sense of the 'semiotic' is the difference which inscribes itself in 'meaning' in the sense of the self-sufficiency of language. For the language of names, the 'semiotic' becomes pure communicability. Inversely, in the 'post-Adamic' languages, that is to say, those which came about after the Fall, in the languages which carry the scar of the injury to the name and for this reason have very little density, the 'semiotic' turns man away from communicability, from the essence of language, from its event. It appears as the meaning of a means of communication. As the independent meaning of communication, the 'semiotic' is inseparable from the 'mimetic'. The 'mimetic' is a non-representative relation of language to another language. It consists of 'correspondences' between entities which resemble each other and gather to create 'communities'. *Semiosis* and *mimesis* constitute the economy of profane languages. If correspondence is communication, a sort of translation which creates the 'magical community' of things, denomination is the translation which transforms this community of 'sensible correspondences' into a community or 'archive' of 'non-sensible correspondences'. In other words: the translation which is operational in denomination is a 'mimetic' transformation whose goal is the recognition of the communicability – of the spirit. The 'mimetic' is not present in the 'semiotic': it appears as a flash, it is the fire, the flame which burns the 'semiotic': 'Rather, the mimetic faculty in language can, like a flame, manifest itself only through a kind of bearer. This bearer is the semiotic element.'[95] The moment the words of language become proper names, words that are singular and without signification, words that do nothing but indicate language's taking-place (depleted of sense if isolated, the proper name is the element of mechanical memory, at least according to Hegel); the moment translations allow the name to show through, language becomes enflamed, it illuminates itself, it strikes the one who seeks 'content' with blindness. It becomes recognisable as language, resembling nothing but itself. There is, according to Benjamin, an image which interrupts history because it shows what has come to pass from the perspective of redemption; this image flashes before our eyes and we are unable to hold it. Language appears in the same way as this image: suddenly and unpredictably, provided the 'mimetic' is the sign of communicability. What does the apparition show? Maybe that history is nothing more than a barely noticeable density of language. It is through this density, by moving through history, that we experience language and the name.

What does thinking of the name as the origin of language tell us about translation? It tells us this: for all translation, what is to

be translated, the words or names of another language, becomes
something that does not yet have a name, which is 'unknown
under its name'. A translation never contents itself with translating what has already been named or translated. Translation
names and, in naming, it marks itself, it marks communicability.
So, in the post-'Adamic' languages, the act of naming always has
the marks of a 'trenchant decision'; Benjamin would say: of an
'over-naming'. If the name were given before naming, denomination would be nothing more than a programmed operation,
we could never experience the name. On the other hand,
naming cannot be an act of absolute and unlimited spontaneity;
denomination can be no more than a coming-to-be-called or a
letting-it-itself-decide: for if the name given were only a name,
if it were nothing more than an arbitrary sign, how could we
experience the name? Benjamin describes this contradictory
structure of denomination – which is also that of translation, of
the *arch-translation* which is involved in all translations – when
he makes it clear that divine denomination is only 'an expression
of the identity of the creative word and the cognising name in
God, not the prior solution to the task that God explicitly
assigns to man himself: that of naming things.'[96] In a passage of
his essay on language, Benjamin quotes a poem which speaks of
a divine sign: God gives a sign to the animals so that they will
approach man to receive their names. This image of the sign
(*Bild des Zeichens*), Benjamin says, translates 'in a an almost
sublime way the linguistic community of mute creation with
God.'[97] Maybe the divine sign constitutes the singularity of each
thing, of each creature: because of it the experience of communicability is always a singular one. But of this sign only a sign
remains for man: the experience of the name, translation.
Heidegger reminds the audience of his lectures on *Was heißt
Denken?*, that in order to translate we must pay attention to the
'saying of words': 'Such a trans*lation* (*übersetzen*) is a *trans*lation
(*Übersetzen*). This *trans*lation (*Übersetzen*) is possible only if we
transpose ourselves into what speaks from these words. And this
transposition succeeds only by a leap (*Sprung*), the leap of a
single vision which sees what the words [...] state, or tell.'[98]
But can we see what is said? Here is Heidegger's answer: 'We
can, provided what is told is more than just the wording
(*Wortlaut*), provided that seeing is more than just the seeing

with the eyes of the body.' This gaze which is not sensible, which perceives the 'saying' of language or words (*Sagen der Worte*) and is essential to translation as passage, as *leap*, as decision, isn't this the gaze whose necessity is shown by the 'sign' or the hint, the gaze kept and watched by the awakened being? Paying attention to the 'saying' of words does not mean paying attention to the results of philology but rather to the *Winke* of language which are the forgotten origins of that science. We must return to historicity to understand the history of languages – which is also the history of the relation between two languages, the history of translation, of '*Über-setzung*' and '*Übersetzung*'. We miss the *Wink* if we refuse historical comprehension.

> Whatever philology (*Sprachwissenschaft*) has to say must first be given to it historically (*geschichtlich*); it must have reached philology by pre-scientific ways leading up to the history of language. Only if history (*Geschichte*) is given, and only then, can the historical subject matter become the subject matter of a historiography (*Historie*), in which data remain by their nature what they are. Here is where we take our 'signs' or hints (*Winke*).[99]

Obviously Heidegger never says that (Benjamin's) God signals. But we could here quote a line of Jean-Luc Nancy's which brings both Hölderlin and Heidegger to mind: 'To "give a sign" is perhaps always – divine.'[100] In any case, for Heidegger there is no translation if we do not pay attention to this 'saying' which signals. Translating the thing, finding a name, is paying attention to the sign of the other, exposing language to the other. Heidegger must always name – by translating – and he always finds names, even when he uses 'current' words, even when he takes up philosophical concepts belonging to the tradition. The 'sign' of the other, the *Wink*, makes us pay attention. The name responds to a call – to its own call – in calling the thing:

> To name something – that is to call it by its name. More fundamentally, to name is to call and clothe something with a word. What is so called is then at the call (*Ruf*) of the

word. What is called appears as what comes to presence (*erscheint als das Anwesende*), and in its presence it is kept, commanded, summoned (*geborgen, befohlen, geheißen*) by the calling word. So, called (*geheißen*) by its name, called into a presence (*in ein Anwesen Gerufene*), it in turn calls. It is named, has the name. By naming, we call on (*heißen*) what is present (*Anwesendes*) to arrive. Arrive where? That remains to be thought about. In any case, all naming and all being named is the familiar 'to call' only because naming itself consists by nature in the proper calling (*Heißen*), in the call to come, in a commanding and a summoning call.[101]

The reader who tries to reconstruct the 'logic' of this argument must draw all its possible conclusions. The one which seems most obvious is that we must think the call, the *Geheiß* and the *heißen*, on the basis of the name – and not just the name on the basis of the call. It is as if the name were in a 'transcendental' position relative to the 'apparition' of the thing, as if being-called meant being-called-by-the-name, as if the name signalled and called itself. Certainly denomination depends on the call: we cannot think denomination without thinking the call. However, isn't it the name or something like a name which calls – the thing? The call allows us to think denomination while already presupposing the name. The name is supposed to have the power to 'keep' (*bergen*) the thing, it can't be just any name. If the *Wink* is the origin of all denomination and all translation, if the *Wink* calls us, signals to us, says to us: you must name the thing, you must give it this name, then we are already called by the name before naming. At the same time, the gaze which recognises the *Wink* of language is a 'leap': naming is the problem of man, and to be able to name one needs a certain 'spontaneity' – Heidegger never uses this word – the 'spontaneity' of a decision. We are thus brought back to the contradictory structure of denomination/translation. Man can leap only because he is called by the name. Let us add: like the divine sign Benjamin speaks of, the *Sage* or *Zeige* which for Heidegger constitutes the essence of language (*Das Wesende der Sprache ist die Sage als die Zeige* ['*The essential being of language is Saying as Showing.*']),[102] designates an originary dimension of 'communicability'. This dimension precedes all apparition and denomination. It is the dimension of the call — of the name. For calling always amounts to showing and showing always amounts to calling, to signalling. Naming, translating, is thus the chance of a gesture, of a sign, of the *Wink, and* of an act, of a decision, of the *Sprung.*

III

Over-naming and melancholy

> But forgetting always involves the best;
> for it involves the possibility of redemption.
> (Walter Benjamin)[103]

In Schelling's *Of Human Freedom*, a melancholic voice evokes the melancholic condition which is at the origin of life:

> In God too there would be a depth of darkness if he did not make the condition his own and unite it to him as one and as absolute personality. Man never gains control over the condition even though in evil he strives to do so; it is only loaned to him independent of him; hence his personality and selfhood can never be raised to complete actuality. This is the sadness which adheres to all finite life, and inasmuch as there is even in God himself a condition at least relatively independent, there is in him, too, a source of sadness which, however, never attains actuality but rather serves for the eternal joy of overcoming. *Hence* the veil of sadness which is spread over all nature, the deep, unappeasable melancholy of all life.[104]

A lack of reflection, the experience of evil and the unrealisable nature of pure actuality are the causes of the melancholic character of man, nature and everything living. Absolute reflection, reflection as appropriation of the condition (*Bedingung*), does not know melancholy: no veil separates ground from existence. The ground does not erect itself as a veil. We can also translate this in terms of a dialectic between nature and spirit: 'Melancholy (*Schwermut*) itself, however, is the historical spirit in its natural depth', Adorno writes of Kierkegaard.[105] The scission of ground and existence calls for the reappropriation of the condition; the separation which lets the spirit sink deeply into its own nature demands the accomplishment of spiritual history. So the problem of creation – how does one reappropriate one's own condition? – would not arise if melancholy were not what Heidegger calls a 'tone' or a 'fundamental tone' (*Grundstimmung*), the source of the lament, of the 'grief of the call'.[106] Heidegger quotes Schelling's sentence about the melancholy of creatures and adds: 'This is why all creators, creative people, the poets, thinkers, and founders of the state, are "melancholy spirits" according to Aristotle.'[107] As in his lectures on the fundamental concepts of metaphysics, Heidegger draws on Aristotle at the moment when he names those who are affected by melancholy. But there is nothing surprising in the fact that for Heidegger the poet, the thinker and the founder of the state are the ultimate melancholics. By opposing creatures' melancholy to a sadness which never becomes actual, by opposing melancholy to the creator's pure act, Schelling seems to privilege melancholic man, as if man were more melancholic than nature: confronted with the problem of creation, with his condition, man passes through evil. It is sufficient to accept this interpretation – melancholy reveals itself in creation, in the act of a finite creator – to attribute melancholy to *Dasein*: for *Dasein* is the locus of creation. Heidegger explains his views of creation in the *Introduction to Metaphysics*:

The *polis* is the historical place, the there *in* which, *out of* which, and *for* which history happens. To this place and scene of history belong the gods, the temples, the priests, the festivals, the games, the poets, the thinkers, the ruler, the council of elders, the assembly of people, the army and the fleet. All this does not first belong to the *polis*, does not become political by entering into a relation with a statesman and a general and the business of the state. No, it is political, i.e. at the site of history, provided there be (for example) poets *alone*, but then really poets, priests *alone*, but then really priests, rulers *alone*, but then really rulers. *Be*, this means: as violent men to use power, to become pre-eminent in historical being as creators, as men of action. Pre-eminent in the historical place, they become at the same time *apolis*,

without city and place, lonely, strange, alien and uncanny
(*Unheimliche*), without issue amid the beings as a whole,
without statute and limit, without structure and order,
because they themselves *as* creators must first create all
this.[108]

Thus melancholy is neither simply political nor purely apoliti-
cal. It already marks a gap in relation to what has been created,
remains attached to what it detaches itself from. As such it
constitutes the *Grundstimmung* which accompanies and divides
action, paralyses and prepares creation. But what is the task of
the founders of history? If foundation transforms the relationship between the people and Being, and if the fate of language
depends on this relationship, mustn't we find the name of this
alliance which precedes all history? Isn't the political act, the
founding act, an act of denomination? Isn't a melancholy determined on the grounds of creation — of creation as self-affirmation — necessarily a reaction which presupposes the lack or loss
of a name, a reaction shared by the impossibility of naming and
the desire to name? Doesn't this experience of melancholy
remain trapped in the 'hubris' that Benjamin defines as the
attempt to give oneself form (*sich selbst Gestalt geben*) and
which, for Schelling, is evil?[109]

As Giorgio Agamben shows along the lines of Freud's analysis, melancholy can also be 'the phantasmatic capacity to make
an object which resists appropriation appear as if lost'.[110] Faithfulness to the object here inscribes itself in a will to reappropriation which corresponds to the 'hubris' of creation. By marking
a distance from what is, melancholy limits the will to reappropriate while clearing a path for it. It binds man to the
contemplation of his powerlessness, but by simulating loss it
accomplishes what creation could not. At the same time,
however, we must be aware of another melancholy: the inappropriable itself, exposed to the will to reappropriation,
becomes melancholic. What about this melancholy? Maybe it is
a melancholic supplement which affects the logic of creation or
reappropriation.

Reading the passage on melancholy in Benjamin's essay on
language as the language of names, we see that he situates
melancholy in nature, in the world of things. It is not man who

is melancholic, which means here that man is melancholic only to the extent that something of melancholic nature, of this melancholy which is not a result of the difficulty of creating, is part of his essence. Can we say that Benjamin is satisfied with performing a simple inversion? That would be true if he claimed, for example, that nature's melancholy is due to the imperfection of man's works or to nature's inability to name, its mutism (*Stummheit*). At first, Benjamin seems to be advancing this kind of argument. But it is only a provisional argument. For the 'metaphysical truth' that imposes itself has a double meaning:

> It is a metaphysical truth that all nature would begin to lament if it were endowed with language. (Though to 'endow with language' is more than to 'make able to speak'.) This proposition has a double meaning. It means, first: she would lament language itself. Speechlessness: this is the great sorrow of nature (and for the sake of her redemption the life and language of *man* — not only, as is supposed, of the poet — are in nature).[111]

How is it possible to reach this metaphysical truth? How can nature, the thing, be endowed with language? How should the relationship between melancholy and language be conceived? We must first make a distinction between melancholic mutism, the mutism 'which we mean by the deep sadness of nature',[112] and this other mutism which is the sign of a certain beatitude (*Seligkeit*) and joyous life. For language itself does not remain what it is. This distinction which divides mutism is necessary because the language of names which translates the language of things loses the ability to name, to translate by naming: it becomes the language of arbitrary signs. Man's own beatitude where his life is in accordance with the 'pure linguistic spirit' (*reiner Sprachgeist*) is separated by a difference of degree from the beatitude of mute, and not melancholic, nature. But no degree of difference can be found in mutism: it is divided by a rupture. To establish a degree of difference, we must presuppose the immanence constituted by a set of relations; but the passage from one language to another, the fall, destroys all immanence.

Mutism is not identical with melancholy. It may not be

melancholic. The loss of the language of things, the impossibility of translating the thing, implies a loss of its essential and originary mutism. Mutism is at once the decisive trait of the language of things, of the thing which receives the name corresponding to it, and the effect of melancholy: 'Because she is mute, nature mourns. Yet the inversion of this proposition leads even further into the essence of nature; the sadness of nature makes her mute.'[113] We hear the lament of nature: but this lament is not the result of a transformation of its mutism. Mutism doesn't need to transform itself into language for us to hear its sigh of lament. Nothing precedes melancholy. Melancholic mutism is a lament and the lament is the wordless word of mutism. Mutism itself speaks of the sadness of the thing by lamenting. The thing becomes confused with melancholic mutism which speaks before speaking: 'even when there is only a rustling of plants, in it there is always a lament.'[114] When mutism speaks and touches upon the limit of language, when it communicates itself – but it is nothing more than this barely noticeable contact, the sound produced by the vibration of a string – it is an effect of the sadness of the thing which has lost its originary mutism, which is no longer mute or is more than mute. As lament mutism reveals an affectivity. The lament is 'the most undifferentiated, impotent expression of language', it 'contains scarcely more than its sensuous breath': at the limit of language, we cannot decide whether we endowed the thing with language or whether the thing itself touched upon it.

Couldn't this logic of melancholy be the one which determines the mutism of sacred joy, of beatitude? Benjamin gives no clue which would allow this hypothesis to be confirmed. But nothing prevents us from thinking that non-melancholic mutism is an effect of sacred joy and happiness. Happiness also strikes us dumb. Adorno has shown that the reflexivity inherent in language abandons happiness to its own past:

> To happiness the same applies as to truth: one does not have it, but is in it. Indeed, happiness is nothing other than being encompassed, an after-image of the original shelter within the mother. But for this reason no-one who is happy can know that he is so. To see happiness, he would have to pass out of it: to be as if already born. He who says he is happy

lies, and in invoking happiness, sins against it. He alone keeps
faith who says: I was happy. The only relation of consciousness to happiness is gratitude: in which lies its incomparable
dignity.[115]

Happiness is, by definition, that which has yet to be born: birth
and language go together. Happiness abandons itself to language
because it is essentially an abandonment; it abandons itself to
that which abandons it to become memory. By expressing itself
in language, happiness remains attached to the past. Radicalising
Adorno's claim, we could say that language is the expression of
happiness, its abandonment and its memory. Only language can
evidence the faithfulness to happiness; this does not mean,
however, that the statement 'I was happy' must be repeated
again and again, since language itself states its own statement.
Language is the inscription of happiness in time. To be faithful
to happiness is not to deny the mark of its expression, the
temporal gap, language. Such a faithfulness manifests itself in
recognition. Language as the expression of past happiness
addresses itself to the other through the pathos of recognition.
This pathos is not pompous. Rosenzweig shows that recognition and the other cannot be measured against each other:
recognition has no object, the other does not become a property
(*Eigentum*) of the one who recognises.[116] But if recognition
forbids representing the other, how can he be addressed? The
memory of recognition demands that representation is abandoned. Otherwise it is in danger of becoming invocation and
thereby revoking happiness. To experience happiness and truth
means perhaps undergoing the linguistic experience of what is
immemorial and unforgettable, of what is immemorial because
it is unforgettable and is unforgettable because it is immemorial.
The immemorial and the unforgettable announce themselves in
this paradoxical experience: the more they suspend language,
the more they remain shot through with it. According to
Adorno, recognition, that which makes us relate to language, is
the sign of the dignity (*Würde*) of happiness. Adorno is very
close to Heidegger here: in his work on *Gelassenheit* Heidegger
suggests that recognition – the recognition of thought – is what
is noble in man's essence (*das Edle seines Wesens*).[117] But if there
is a connection between recognition and happiness, if this

connection determines the dignity of happiness, we will not be at all surprised to see that Benjamin, when he speaks of the beatitude of nature, quotes a line which names a certain dignity, the nobility of animals: 'Friedrich Müller has Adam say about the animals that leave him after he has named them, "And saw by the nobility (*Adel*) with which they leaped away from me that man had given them a name."'[118] Isn't the nobility in question here the dignity which recognition bestows upon the one who knows or has known happiness and joy? Certainly, nature which has been named remains mute: but it remains mute because the recognition which appears to bestow the title of its nobility upon it makes no reference to the past. The language of names envelops nature, it is its happiness and truth, not the time of that happiness and truth.

Nature named, called by its own name, is joyous. But this joy is not without contamination by sorrow. It is joyous nature that mourns, not nature betrayed by man, the nature that man scorns by scorning the language of names. Joyous nature is also melancholic nature. This claim seems incompatible with Benjamin's argument. How do we explain a movement that puts nature in contradiction with itself? A hesitation becomes noticeable in the text, as if Benjamin was compelled to follow two different leads, leads which go in opposite directions. Mutism points to nature's mourning: 'In all mourning sadness (*Trauer*) there is the deepest inclination to speechlessness (*Sprachlosigkeit*).' Just as endowing something with language is much more than enabling something to speak, losing speech, no longer speaking, 'is infinitely more than inability or disinclination to communicate'. Only that which has lost speech can be endowed with language: the lament does not refer to an inability or to a disinclination which would affect the possibility of communicating. It refers to denomination: 'That which mourns feels itself thoroughly known by the unknowable. To be named – even when the one who names is god-like and blissful – perhaps always remains an intimation of mournful sadness (*Trauer*). But how much more so when the name received does not stem from the blessed, paradisiac language of names, but from the hundred languages of man, in which the name has already withered, yet which, according to God's pronouncement, have knowledge of things.'[119] This passage – which also suggests that the relation between name and knowledge is asymmetric: but which knowledge? – has the characteristic of a real passage: we pass from one level to another without noticing. Benjamin begins by saying that the melancholy of nature – of the named thing – is caused by the proper name, for the unknowable – God – recognises what he creates completely: 'Things have no proper name except in God.' The name itself, in its deepest essence, in its divine essence, already contains melancholy. It is as if melancholy were originary. Benjamin seems to subscribe to a universal proposition: that which receives a name, which is called by its proper name, is melancholic since the name is always and without exception a kind of identification. But by adding a bracketed comment to this proposition which limits its reach, he *simultaneously* situates it at a level which must be distinguished from other levels. Saying that such a proposition is valid for all languages, even the language of names, is to implicitly deny its validity for divine language – even as a suspicion inevitably begins to displace this negation. The sentence 'things have no proper name except in God' takes on a completely different meaning. We must also take a third precision into account. In the language of arbitrary signs, the natural life of the name comes to an end. The name is already withered, it has become external to itself. This artificial language wants to communicate something which is elsewhere: 'In stepping outside the purer language of names, man makes language a means (that is, a knowledge inappropriate to him), and therefore also, in one part at any rate, a *mere* sign.'[120] Thus, it is above all referential language which is supposed to cause melancholy. It is at the origin of the multiplicity and confusion of languages: 'There is in the relation of human languages to that of things, something that can be described as "over-naming": over-naming as the deepest linguistic reason for all melancholy and (from the point of view of things) of all muteness.'[121]

And so Benjamin goes from one extreme to the other. On the one hand nature is melancholic to the degree that it is over-named and so no longer has a proper name; on the other hand, this over-naming is already determined by the proper name, by denomination. From this perspective, all naming is over-naming. A difference which is not a difference of degree inscribes itself in the universality of the rule, and enables us to invert the terms. If all naming is over-naming, all over-naming is naming. Over-naming must keep the trace of a name which is not already indebted or which has settled its account, otherwise there would be no naming. The thing laments over-naming, it laments the name without lamenting. A name can be imperfect relative to a perfection it does not reach. But if over-naming is general, no name is ever imperfect. The name is neither perfect nor imperfect, neither fitting nor inadequate. The language of names translates and does not translate the language of things. Benjamin causes the meaning of the rule to stray. The rule strays. This straying can take the form of a hesitation: we can accuse Benjamin of not being rigorous enough. But the same straying may also show us the path to follow to think another rigour. This rigour does not measure itself against a fixed generality: it presents itself as the rigour of a rule which can only constitute itself as a rule if it engenders its own difference, a difference which escapes regulation. What this rule designates is the possibility and the necessity of a double interpretation of melancholy, of the passage from one melancholy to another. (1) If over-naming is nothing more than a terrible accident, if it does not regulate naming in general, nature can be melancholic only because of a failure. Man has failed language. Even if we maintain that he couldn't have done otherwise and that the language of names already fails divine language – Benjamin does not exclude this idea – we continue to think of melancholy as a reaction to man's condition. Nature is melancholic because man is unable to appropriate his own condition. It does nothing more than reflect man's melancholy, it speaks, it laments under the melancholic gaze of man, who is unable to give it its proper name. (2) On the other hand, if over-naming is universal, if it regulates naming, the melancholy of nature is no longer subject to the condition of man. It results from the very structure of the name and is not derived from a lack, or an imperfection, or a failure – at least if we define lack on the basis of an essence without lack. Naming more than it names, the name not only never appropriates what it names, it is never able to assure its own identity. It is excessive, for essential reasons: it must be excessive so that it can name the thing. It is thus meaningless to say that this excess is equivalent to a lack – to the lack of plenitude.

The inappropriable is in this case the essence of appropriation.

It is not in the least what distinguishes a finite from an infinite appropriation. But what is inappropriable, what is immemorial, always already forgotten and in that way unforgettable? The name, language itself, or rather its being given, this gift which is erased as soon as it appears. The melancholy of the thing makes us think about the gift of language, language as gift.

We understand now the complexity of the phrase 'to endow with language'. What language can we give the thing if it laments the over-naming inherent to naming? Benjamin says that endowing something with language is much more than making it capable of speech: is it making it capable of transmitting its spiritual essence, language itself, communicability? Benjamin calls this transmission translation. So is endowing with language translating? No. We have just seen that endowing with language is not in the least concerned with translating the spiritual essence attributed to the thing, with naming it. If all translation endows the other with language, endowing with language does not necessarily equal translating the language of the other. By using language to lament, by becoming a lament itself, the thing strips language away until only its most rudimentary form remains. The thing remains other while calling for language: its alterity is not the other of language. How can we translate a lament? The thing shows what does not allow itself to be seen, the inappropriable. However, we must not forget that the thing has its own language and that its spiritual essence manifests itself in its communicability. Its language precedes the language of names. It awaits and refuses translation. Mutism, this mutism that is the buried ground of the lament, thus places the thing at the very heart of language – of names: the thing prescribes the over-naming which it laments. It reveals itself to be the inappropriable or the incommunicable, what shows itself without showing itself in melancholy. But the inappropriable is not at all a secret, like the passwords that constitute the language of nature. For this reason, it shatters the unity of the linguistic movement whose origin it is:

> The language of an entity is the medium in which its spiritual essence is communicated. The uninterrupted flow of this communication runs through the whole of nature from the lowest forms of existence to man and from man to God.

Man communicates himself to God through the name, which he gives to nature and (in proper names) to his own kind; to nature he gives names according to the communication that he receives from her, for the whole of nature, too, is imbued with a nameless, unspoken language, the residue of the creative word of God, which is preserved in man as the cognising name and above man as the judgement suspended over him. The language of nature is comparable to a secret password (*geheime Losung*) that each sentry passes to the next in his own language, but the meaning of the password is the sentry's language itself. All higher languages are a translation of those lower, until in ultimate clarity the word of God unfolds, which is the unity of this *linguistic* movement.[122]

The thing which laments does not turn into an allegory, if turning into an allegory means being invested with meaning; that is to say, being exposed to what comes from outside and receiving, under the melancholic gaze of the other, a meaning which remains exterior and alien. That is how Benjamin defines allegory in his study of the origins of German tragic drama:

If the object becomes allegorical under the gaze of melancholy, if melancholy causes life to flow out of it and it remains dead, but eternally secure, then it is exposed to the allegorist, it is unconditionally in his power. That is to say it is now quite incapable of emanating any meaning or significance of its own; such significance as it has, it acquires from the allegorist. He places it within it, and stands behind it; not in a psychological but in an ontological sense. In his hands the object becomes something different; through it he speaks of something different and for him it becomes a key to the realm of hidden knowledge; and he reveres it as the emblem of this. This is what determines the character of allegory as a form of writing. It is a schema; and as a schema it is an object of knowledge, but it is not securely possessed until it becomes a fixed schema: at one and the same time a fixed image and a fixating sign.[123]

The allegorical transformation repeats the transformation of the language of names into referential language; hence the essential difference between the melancholy of nature and of man. To call the sadness of nature melancholy presupposes a definition of melancholy which emphasises the resistance this sadness offers to allegorical intention. The thing which laments does not become an allegory because the lament does not allow itself to be reduced to its representation or schematic appropriation. As lament, the thing does not stand in the actuality of the life of meaning, but equally it does not lend itself to fixation, abstraction or reification. The lament is neither symbolic nor allegorical, it preserves the thing both from the idealisation operated by the symbol and from the mortification which it must suffer to become an object of knowledge and criticism: 'Criticism means the mortification of the works.'[124] In his analysis of allegory, Paul de Man stresses the rupture that opposes allegory to metaphor. This rupture determines the meaning of allegory: a metaphor is the result of a synthesis of the literal and figurative meanings carried out by the power of a resemblance while an allegory suggests a figurative meaning which marks an absolute distance from any literal meaning. Allegorical substitution destroys all resemblance, all correspondence.[125] Benjamin deduces the scriptural character proper to allegory from this destruction: even if in a later text he conceives of a writing which concentrates and assembles the power of resemblance within itself, the mimetic power of language, here he does not hesitate to assign writing to death. Writing deprives *mimesis* of all its power. So, from the moment that all naming is over-naming, the writing that freezes the thing and runs up against the lament inscribes itself in the thing. The lament prescribes over-naming: naming is always more than naming because the lament always adds itself to the name. But the prefix *over* also indicates allegorical inscription, it is the indissociable sign of allegory and what exceeds its writing. In other words: the supplement of denomination, the name as supplement, does not have a single indivisible meaning. Over-naming is both the allegory of language and the indecision which suspends allegory, symbol and metaphor. Thus it is not surprising that Benjamin returns to the idea of a melancholy linked to over-naming in the context of his theory of allegory. He repeats the passage on the mutism of nature from his work on language word for word and emphasises the allegorical value of over-naming: 'To be named – even if the one who names is god-like and blissful –

perhaps always remains an intimation of mournful sadness. But how much more so not to be named, only to be read, to be read uncertainly by the allegorist, and to have become highly significant thanks only to him.'[126] Allegory substitutes meaning for naming: reading is the exhaustion of naming, absolute over-naming. We can consider allegorical melancholy to be reactive melancholy: it actually aims for the reappropriation of the condition through allegory. But that would be to stop its movement. For if it is impossible to fix the meaning of the supplement, it is equally impossible to block the passage between one meaning and another.

The mournful sadness and melancholy of the thing mark a limit for allegory. Does that mean that there is a link between this melancholy and tragedy? Benjamin never ceases to point out the fundamental differences that forbid identifying the experience of tragedy with that of melancholy. Maybe we have to start by excluding melancholic mutism from the tragic mutism dealt with in the book on the *Trauerspiel*. In order to approach the essence of tragic mutism, Benjamin first quotes a passage from *The Star of Redemption* where Rosenzweig shows that silence (*Schweigen*) is the very essence of tragedy. For Rosenzweig there would be no tragedy if the hero did not fall silent. His mutism, his silence, is his language. In referring to Rosenzweig, Benjamin chooses a starting point for a reflection on the language of tragedy which also appeals to other witnesses, Lukács and Nietzsche. This reflection is summed up in the following sentences:

> The greater the discrepancy between the tragic word and the situation – which can no longer be called tragic when there is no discrepancy – the more surely has the hero escaped the ancient statutes. The instant they finally overtake him, he throws only the dumb shadow of his being, the self, as a sacrifice, while his soul finds refuge in the word of a distant community [...] Tragic silence, far more than tragic pathos, became the storehouse of an experience of the sublimity of linguistic expression.[127]

In tragedy, speech is always late when compared with the situation. It is this delay, it is death as the most extreme experience of a destitute being, of a being completely condemned to a physical existence without speech, which confers speech upon those who have refused to share it. The hero must sacrifice his self, the mute shadow of his being, because of his refusal. The word is the gift of silence, of mutism: a sacrifice which leads to rebirth. Over-naming is also a delay. But in the context of universal over-naming, it is not a question of the name just being late, as if it only had to catch up with the named to no longer be delayed. The name is late in relation to itself. As a *given* name it is its own delay. That explains why the *Stimmung* which arises in the delay (*Traurigkeit, Trauer*) and is nothing other than this delay, must be recognised as *Grundstimmung*, as an other melancholy or as a melancholy of the other. (Sadness and melancholy are indissociable. Melancholy is nothing but a certain intensity of sadness: 'For whereas in the realm of the emotions it is not unusual for the relation between an intention and its object to alternate between attraction and repulsion, mournful sadness is capable of a special intensification, a progressive deepening of its intention. Pensiveness [*Tiefsinn*] is characteristic above all of the melancholic and mournful.'[128] When Benjamin speaks of sadness, we cannot but hear the lament of the melancholic. The values associated with the concepts of *Traurigkeit, Trauer, Tiefsinn* and *Melancholie* are interchangeable.) However, the over-naming which causes melancholy is not unrelated to tragic experience: 'Over-naming as the linguistic being of what is sad (*des Traurigen*) points to another peculiar relation of language: the one which links it to the over-determination prevailing in the tragic relationship between the languages of human speakers.'[129] How can we justify this usage of the term 'tragic'? Benjamin does not clarify his use of the concept of tragedy in his text on the language of names. We have to look elsewhere: the book on the *Trauerspiel* and two essays seem to give important clues. One essay is entitled '*Trauerspiel* and Tragedy', the other 'The Role of Language in *Trauerspiel* and Tragedy'.[130] Like the text on the language of names, they were written in 1916. Benjamin states at the beginning of the second essay that the concept of the tragic is based on the laws of dialogue. A poem, a novel, an event cannot be called tragic. The tragic 'is the only form proper to human dialogue (*menschliche Wechselrede*)'.[131] Being tragic, dialogue is never sad. For not bringing itself into the order of language is the 'deepest and indeed only expression' of what is sad (*das Traurige*). Sadness (*Trauer*), Benjamin says, 'unlike tragedy, is not a ruling force. It is not the indissoluble law of inescapable orders that prevails in tragedy. It is merely a feeling (*Gefühl*).' The feeling of sadness is thus found to be opposed to language whose purity turns out to be tragic: 'It is the pure word (*das reine Wort*) itself that has an immediate tragic force.'

In its purity, in its immediacy, language is tragic because it entails a decision. Decision as a characteristic of pure and immediate language remains alien to sadness. A lament never decides anything, whereas 'every speech in the tragedy is tragically decisive'. If the text on the significance of language in *Trauerspiel* and tragedy shows the meaning of tragedy, the meaning which it acquires inasmuch as it stands for the meaning of a decision that language will always already have taken, the essay on the language of names describes the genealogy of this meaning. It tells the story of the immediacy and purity of the language of decision, of the word which judges (*das richtende Wort*). Language is decisive, it deploys 'the autonomous laws of human discourse' because it has the form and reflects the obviousness of a judgement. We meet a stranger and we judge him immediately: this experience teaches us that we cannot do otherwise than judge. There may be no language other than that of art that can suspend the language of judgement, and it is because of this that it has been possible to say that poetry is close to the language of names. Benjamin makes it clear that judgement presupposes the loss of the language of names. It is linked to the knowledge of good and evil. This knowledge turns out to be identical with referential language, with the positioning of a referent outside language. The multiplicity of languages is the result, the inseparable consequence, of language going outside of itself. To become a position and to become multiple: that is the destiny of language and those who speak. The knowledge of good and evil substitutes itself for the knowledge of things based on names. Knowledge of good and evil is just knowledge separated from the name; and if human languages still know things it is because over-naming must be naming so that it does not abolish itself. Referential language is no less 'magical' than the language of names: but exteriority belongs to its magic. By going outside of itself, language continues to name; it names something which no longer stands in its immanence, in 'that contemplation (*Anschauen*) of things in which their language passes into man.'[132] Language draws attention to itself, it becomes 'expressly' magical. We would be tempted to say that black magic enchants language: it triumphs over white magic in an inevitable confrontation. Judgement (*Gericht*) is the 'purification and elevation' of the language whose magic founds itself upon an immediacy affected by a non-linguistic outside. To name something outside language signifies knowledge of good and evil: 'the judging word has direct knowledge of good and evil. Its magic is different from that of the name, but equally magical.'[133] The loss of the language of names is not at all the loss of language itself: it is simultaneously a destruction and restitution of the magical immediacy which characterises language. Judgement comes from the wound inflicted on the name: its magic (*Magie des Urteils*) 'no longer rests blissfully in itself'.[134] Benjamin seems to speak of magic because of this immediacy which always belongs to language, which prevents man from mastering it completely when he turns it into a means. Language judges. It judges the other, its reference, and it is itself the judge who judges the speaker. For this reason, it is decisive, it entails a decision, it has already decided man's fate. Language is the judgement (*Gericht*) which has condemned man to judge the other (*Urteil, richtendes Wort*). But it cannot refer to an object which conceals itself from intuition without presupposing something which has always existed outside of it and, as the origin of abstraction, is also the origin of all allegory:

> For good and evil, being unnameable, nameless, stand outside the language of names, which man leaves behind precisely in the abyss opened by this question. With regard to existing language, the name offers only the ground in which its concrete elements are rooted. But the abstract elements of language – we may perhaps surmise – are rooted in the word of judgement. The immediacy (which, however, is the linguistic root) of the communicability of abstraction resides in judgement. This immediacy in the communication of

abstraction came into being as judgement, when, in the fall, man abandoned immediacy in the communication of the concrete, name, and fell into the abyss of the mediateness of all communication, of the word as means, as the empty word, into the abyss of prattle. For – it must be said again – the question as to good and evil in the world after creation was empty prattle. The tree of knowledge did not stand in the garden of God in order to dispense information on good and evil, but as an emblem of judgement over the questioner. This immense irony marks the mythical origin of law.[135]

Over-naming thus refers to the 'mythical violence' that Benjamin analyses in another essay entitled 'For a Critique of Violence' (1920–1) which deals with the mythical origins of law: 'If mythical violence is law-making, divine violence is law-destroying; if the former sets boundaries, the latter boundlessly destroys them; if mythical violence brings at once guilt and retribution, divine power only expiates; if the former threatens, the latter strikes; if the former is bloody, the latter is lethal without spilling blood.'[136] To introduce laws is to limit. Heidegger reminds us that decisions are always taken at or on a limit; by definition they involve limits and the absence of limits (*Nur an den Grenzen fallen die Entscheidungen, die immer solche sind über Grenzen und Grenzenlosigkeit*).[137] The limitless (*grenzenlos*) destruction Benjamin speaks of in relation to 'divine violence' would consequently be a destruction of the language of decision which decides upon the limit and its absence (*Grenzenlosigkeit*). Mythical violence and judgement are the answers to the questions 'What is good?' and 'What is evil?' In other words, knowledge of good and evil is equivalent to the tragic experience of language. Over-naming refers to the originary presence of judgement which performs the abstraction and allows us to judge instead of name. Its effect is not simply one of contamination: its purity is that of judgement. There is contamination here, but it is the contamination of one purity by another. The relationship between human languages is tragic – and mythical – because each language judges the other. When we hear the lament of nature we move from judgement to the gift of the name, beyond good and evil: this gift already implies over-naming, judgement, but its trace equally resists being erased.[138]

Doesn't the purity of judging language manifest itself in signification? Mustn't we admit that pure signification is necessarily decisive? Where language only signifies, each word is subject to and submits to necessity. The signification of tragic language consists of the signification of language: 'When language has an impact by virtue of its meaning, that impact is tragic. The word as the pure bearer of its meaning is the pure word.'[139] Maybe we have to think of the language of names as one which does not oppose interior to exterior, abstract to concrete: that is why its signification is a signification without signification. It is neither decisive nor necessary – but equally it is not arbitrary or uncertain. From this perspective, signification turns naming into over-naming. Tragic signification is placed under the law of judgement: its purity corresponds to the purity of a 'fulfilled individual time' which is to be distinguished from 'messianic time'. In the essay on *Trauerspiel* and tragedy, Benjamin opposes mechanical to historical time and the empirical to the idea. The possibility of the tragic depends on a time which is neither mechanical nor historical nor messianic:

Historical time, however, differs from this mechanical time. It determines much more than the possibility of spatial changes of a specific magnitude and regularity – think of the hands of a clock – and also more than the possibility of spatial changes of a more complex nature. And without specifying what goes beyond this, what else determines historical time – in short, without defining how it differs from mechanical time – we may assert that the determining force of historical time cannot be fully grasped by, or wholly concentrated in, any empirical process. Rather a process that is perfect in historical terms is quite indeterminate empirically; it is in fact an idea. The idea of fulfilled time is the dominant historical idea of the Bible: it is the idea of messianic time. Moreover, the idea of a fulfilled historical time is never identical with the idea of an individual time. This feature naturally changes the meaning of fulfilment completely, and it is this that distinguishes tragic time from messianic time. Tragic

time is related to the latter in the same way that an individu-
ally fulfilled time relates to a divinely fulfilled one.[140]

Defining individual time as fulfilled is paradoxical: the tragic
hero becomes the victim of this paradox. His immortality leads
him to death; Benjamin calls this death an 'ironic immortality'.
It is the origin of 'tragic irony'. If every event is nothing more
than a function of fulfilled time, of mortal immortality, if
signification commands every event, tragic irony comes to its
most singular expression at the moment when destiny strikes
the hero in his passivity, in his inactivity: 'Tragic time bursts
open, so to speak, like a flower whose calyx emits the astringent
perfume of irony.' The hero's fault consists in individuation.
Individuation institutes the predominance of signification so
that the existence of the individual is marked beforehand by the
possibility and the necessity of a fault. But Benjamin warns us:
we must not define individuation on the basis of its relation
with man. The essence of the individual does not partake of the
individual, as Heidegger would say. What if we had to think
individuation in its essential relationship with language? What if
it weren't individuation which instituted signification but signification which carried, as its major effect, individuation? And
what if the relation between human languages, whose multiplicity seems to be in accordance with the principle of individuation, were tragic – tragically over-determined – because of the
over-determination caused by the signification of each
language? The temporal character of the tragic lets itself be
shaped because everything that comes to pass in individual time
is destined to signification, which is to say over-determination
(*übergroße Determiniertheit, äußerste Determiniertheit, Überbes-
timmtheit*). Tragedy is the representation of individual time: it
operates the passage between this time and dramatic time, it is
the form which the mythical universality of the historical time
of the individual takes. This form cannot be open. *Trauerspiel*,
on the other hand, is based on repetition. Its form is that of the
hyperbole, of a presence which is forever deferred and as a
result ghostly.

The mourning play (*Trauerspiel*) is mathematically comparable to one branch of a hyperbola whose other branch lies in

infinity. The law governing a higher life prevails in the
restricted space of an earthly existence, and all play, until
death puts an end to the game, so as to repeat the same
game, albeit on a grander scale, in another world. It is this
repetition on which the law of the mourning play is
founded. Its events are allegorical schemata, symbolic mirror-
images of a different game. We are transported into that
game by death. The time of the mourning play is not fulfilled, but nevertheless it is finite. It is nonindividual, but
without historical universality. The mourning play is in
every respect a hybrid form. The universality of its time is
spectral, not mythic.[141]

This hyperbolic structure which defers presence and gives
Trauerspiel its game-like character may also control the poly-
morphism of melancholy, what Aristotle describes as the fluctu-
ating power of black bile.[142] Tragedy thus distinguishes itself
through a time which is summed up in a totality – the totality
of a 'unified form' (*geschlossene Form*) – and by a language petri-
fied by signification, while *Trauerspiel* is characterised by a time
which is repetition and by a language which is essentially transformation. 'The word in the process of change is the linguistic
principle of the mourning play.'[143] In the *Trauerspiel* language is
only a form of the language of the word (*Wort*). The word does
and does not belong to language.

Words have a pure emotional life cycle in which they purify
themselves by developing from the natural sound to the pure
sound of feeling. For such words, language is merely a transi-
tional phase within the entire cycle of its transformation, and
in them the mourning play finds its voice. It describes the
path from natural sound via lament to music. In the mourning play, sounds are laid out symphonically, and this constitutes the musical principle of its language and the dramatic
principle of its breaking up and splitting into characters. The
mourning play is nature that enters the purgatory of language only for the sake of the purity of its feelings; it was
already defined in the ancient wise saying that the whole of
nature would begin to lament if it were but granted the gift
of language. For the mourning play does not describe the

motion through the spheres that carries feeling from the pure world of speech out to music and then back to the liberated sorrow of blissful feeling. Instead, midway through its journey nature finds itself betrayed by language, and that powerful blocking (*ungeheuere Hemmung*) of feeling turns to sorrow.

In this passage, once again we find the idea of a melancholic nature, of a nature which laments if it is endowed with speech. Feeling must pass through language to be pure: the purification of natural sound which transforms it into pure feeling is dependent on language. But the circle doesn't close: the natural sound never returns to itself because language interrupts its movement. Nothing can go through language without being led astray. Language seems to be divided: there is an 'emotional life', a passion of language – of the word – and a signification which prevents this passion from reaching its essence. For feeling is the essence of natural sound. The natural sound is an impure feeling. The unity that language 'achieves through feeling unfolding in words', through 'the concentration of the infinite resonance of its sound',[144] stands in opposition to the unity established by the 'eternal inflexibility of the spoken word'. Signification brings ambiguity into language. And it is man who betrays nature: his usurpation of power is what creates 'impassive historical time'. Benjamin writes: 'Thus, with the ambiguity of the word, its *signifying* character, nature falters, and whereas the created world wished only to pour forth in all purity, it was man who bore its crown.'[145] Melancholy – from this perspective, at least – comes from a straying of feeling. In other words: the inhibition which prevents the transformation of the passionate word and turns feeling into melancholy – melancholy is neither pure nor impure, it is neither a natural sound nor the pure sound of feeling – refers to an internal division of language which, as it folds back onto itself, opens up another world, the tragic world. Feeling is always melancholic because language always signifies. Thus, melancholy appears as a kind of originary symptom. In his book on the *Trauerspiel*, Benjamin describes meaning as an inescapable disease (*unentrinnbare Krankheit*). But feeling eventually identifies itself with itself: against the background of the affective unity of language 'sorrow enters into the language of pure feeling – in other words, music'.[146]

How can we express the internal division of language in relation to the problem of denomination? What about the link between language and music? Adorno speaks of a dialectic of music and language:

> The language of music is quite different from all signifying language. It contains a theological dimension. What it says remains concealed in its very utterance, while at the same time being precise and determinate: the message is both clear and veiled. The idea of this utterance is represented by the figure of the divine Name. Such language is a prayer, transformed by the process of demythologisation, i.e. a prayer rid of any magic seeking to exert an influence. It is the human attempt, doomed perhaps, to name the Name itself, not to confer meaning upon it. Music aspires to be a language without intention. But the demarcation line between this language and the language of intentions is not absolute; we are not confronted by two wholly separate realms. There is a dialectic at work. Music is permeated through and through with intentionality. Music bereft of all intentionality (*Meinen*), the merely phenomenal linking of sounds, would be an acoustic parallel to the kaleidoscope. As absolute intentionality, however, it would cease to be music and would effect a false transformation into language. Intentions are central to music, but only intermittently.[147]

Benjamin ascribes to music the power to gather a pure and non-signifying language, a language which isn't, after all, the language of names since it is brought into being by a division which also engenders signifying language – the language of names is supposed to precede all division. Music would then be both the anticipation of a restored language of names and the trace or memory of melancholy. Adorno recognises in music a movement which seeks to name the divine name and must remain attached (dialectic and intermittence, dialectic *as* intermittence) to signification, to intention, to language, to thought which draws near to music in so far as it relies on that which escapes the 'cognitive function': 'To think philosophically means as much as to think intermittences, to be interrupted by that which is not the thought itself.'[148] Each time we assume that the essential (the language of names, the divine name) has been lost. But if over-naming is universal, allowing signification and what remains heterogeneous with regard to the name to inscribe itself into language, then music or, to be even more precise, what in music partakes of melancholy, shows the essential and irreducible straying which separates the gift from the name. Man's melancholy invests things with meaning: man betrays the world but he also betrays things. However, this melancholy, at its extreme, touches the thing itself. It saves mortified things, it hears their lament, their breath; maybe it is this hearing which transforms the lament into music: music which from then on lets the immemorial and unforgettable gift of language be heard. Melancholic man reaches the limit of his humanity, if his *humanitas* consists in the task of denomination. Thus, the analysis of the thing's sadness allows this limit upon which denomination always suspends itself to appear: 'Melancholy betrays the world for the sake of knowledge. But in its tenacious self-absorption it embraces dead objects in its contemplation, in order to redeem them.'[149]

Grundstimmung der Trauer. As *Grundstimmung* melancholy does not oppose itself to what we would think of as its opposite. For if it makes one think of the immemorial gift or, better yet, the retreat of the gift into the name, it is also the *Grundstimmung* which corresponds to a generosity. Maybe this is what Heidegger wanted to show when he spoke of a creative trait *within* melancholy, inside *Trauer*:

> For a calculating understanding, renouncement is a giving away and a loss: real renouncement, in other words one which carries and produces a fundamental tone and deploys itself authentically, is a power of creation and engendering. By letting go of its old possessions it receives a gift, but not after the fact, as a reward; for within it the mournful endurance of necessary renouncement and giving away is a 'receiving'.[150]

The creative trait (*schöpferisch-erzeugend*) is expressed here by the fact of receiving a gift, which also reminds us of the structure of

conception and spontaneity that Benjamin analyses when study-
ing denomination. If the creative trait is what in and through
the *Grundstimmung* inclines renouncement to receive the gift –
the unreceivable – can we then separate it from a denomination
which recognises the thing or makes it appear? The creative
trait divides itself, and it is this division which marks the
passage from naming to over-naming, from over-naming to
naming, from one melancholy to another.

The last part of Benjamin's collection *Berliner Kindheit* ('A
Berlin Childhood') is entitled 'The Little Hunchback'. The
author writes:

> Where he appeared, I could only look at the debris. A tardy
> contemplation, which things escaped; in one year my garden
> had turned into a small garden, my room into a small room
> and my bench into a little bench. They shrunk, and it was as
> if they were growing a hump which now made them part of
> the Little Hunchback's world, and for a long time. This little
> man always arrived before me. And in doing so he blocked
> my path. But other than that he didn't do anything, this
> provost dressed in grey, he just took forgetting's half of
> everything I got. 'If I want to go into my small room / To
> eat my small dinner / There is a Little Hunchback / Who has
> already eaten half!' So the Little Hunchback was often there.
> Only I never saw him. It was always him who watched me.
> And the more piercing his gaze was, the less I saw myself.[151]

The little hunchback keeps the unforgettable and, for that very
reason, forces us to forget the thing: to forget that we have
forgotten. Isn't he the emblematic image of what makes originary melancholy come forth? Every time we name the thing, the
little hunchback watches us: the hump is the mark of over-
naming. But we never see the one who watches and abandons
us. *Und lauschst du noch dem trauervollen Zeichen ...*

IV

Apparitions

The unreadable name

Memory and promise – can we think them without experiencing the name? What does this experience consist of? The appearance of a name is never without a certain promise, even if we are hearing the name for the first time. Every time a name appears for the first time. The name is a beginning, and as such it is intimidating. But at the same time, its being-a-beginning or its being-*at-the*-beginning draws us to it. What can we expect if we hear the name of the other for the first time, if we have no memory of that name? Nothing. But we would be unable to hear that name, or any other, if the name did not have a strange power of evocation. In a text on Bloch from 1965, Adorno describes his name as 'dark as a gateway'[152] (*dunkel wie ein Tor*): maybe because of the vowel which takes the shape of an open mouth or hole (*Loch*) and the consonants which surround it like two columns. Through this transcription of a 'tonal figure' (*Klangfigur*), Adorno tries to verbalise his audio-visual impression. The name of the philosopher, its phono-graphic figure, impresses itself upon him *before* he has read the book which has this name on its cover. It is a youthful or first experience, the experience of the name as the origin of experience. And it is not insignificant that the motto Adorno chooses for his text expresses astonishment. It does so in one of Adorno's languages, the one he attributes elsewhere[153] to his native town, the *Dialekt meiner Vaterstadt*. *Vaterstadt*, his father's town, not *Heimatstadt* – this passage, written in 1945, deals with language and what can happen to it in the misery of exile, as if the father avenged himself by imposing a dialect on the one who tries to keep the memory of his language whole, a foreign language in a foreign country, raped in its native land. Isn't wanting to keep one's language wanting to keep the name of that language, the name which is the 'prototype' of thought *in* languages and which makes German untranslatable? German is more philosophical than other languages (as Adorno claims in his answer to the question *Was ist deutsch?*): consequently, it stays nearest to the name. Here is the epigraph, the sentence written in the Frankfurt tongue, a variation of Hesse's dialect: *Ui, haww' ich gesacht* ('Wow ... I said'). The irony of this epigraph names the name. An epigraph always operates in the same way as a name.

Names carry memory, even if we have never heard them before. Because of this, names promise and can be taken as promises: after the name appears, we are waiting for something. The name, 'dark as a gateway', invites us to cross a limit by appearing. It appears when we aren't expecting it. In his essay on language, Benjamin alludes to the 'intuition' of 'mythological wisdom' according to which 'man's name is his fate'.[154] Is it conceivable that the name could be the archive of all memory? The name promises the hearer, the other, a knowledge that the bearer of the name has already forgotten: he must have forgotten it to become what he is, but also to respond and to be responsible. 'The man with a proper name is the only one who can open his mouth and reply to the divine call', says Rosenzweig. We are judged by the name, we are pre-judged, and this judgement is a sort of death warrant because it says the inevitable. As soon as we start to be, to be named, as soon as we are called to appear, we hide, we try to escape from the revelatory force, the memory, the truth of the name. The possibility of survival, of another memory and another promise, thus depends on a certain unreadability: but an essential and not accidental unreadability. The name must be essentially unreadable. We can save ourselves or be saved only if something in the name remains unreadable. The name remains unreadable in so far as it is a promise; but for the name to be a promise and to carry memory it has to be given, it has to appear as a gift. This gift, as we will see, is the event of language.

The gift of language

'Apparition': the inverted commas indicate that the concept is loaded with meanings. It can refer to the apparition of a presence, to the apparition that makes presence manifest, to the appearance of that which is presented, etc. But the inverted commas also refer to Adorno. What he calls 'apparition' has the same structure as the name, the proper name, the name itself. What can we properly say about the name? What can we say about it that would be improper? Is the name properly the name? To answer these questions I will draw on Benjamin again, on his 'theologico-political' thought and his digressions on language in general and the language of man. (They are indeed 'digressions': they do not seem to lead in the same direction as the *conventional* theory of language, of which Benjamin says that it is in accordance with a 'bourgeois' idea or concept. A surprising affirmation, since he does not deal with the socio-political implications of language in his early essay. Maybe we should read the text in question as a 'pre-history' [*Urgeschichte*] of these implications. Which, obviously, does not explain the specificity of the era encompassed by a 'bourgeois concept' of language.) In the course of his digressions, Benjamin identifies three languages, or rather three different states of language: God's language, paradisiacal human language and language as a 'parody' of God's language. God's language is the one which gives names to what has just been created by the word, by the 'creating word' (*das schaffende Wort*), this word which allows itself to be neither spoken nor written, neither classified nor translated, neither chosen nor refused, neither loved nor hated, since it absolutely precedes all other tongues and languages. There is no gap between the word and the name which God gives to created things (*der erkennende Name*: it recognises the created thing as such): the two move in the same circle, in the circle of divine sameness, they intertwine, intersect and interchange: 'In God the name is creative because it is word, and God's word is cognisant (*Gottes Wort ist erkennd*) because it is a name.'[155] In the name God recognises himself as creator, as word. He recognises, through the name, the creation which would be unknowable without name: 'God made things knowable in their names. Man, however, names them according to knowledge.'[156] Knowledge is linked to the name – and to its forgetting. God recognises creation through the name and in that way recognises himself in his 'linguistic essence'. But divine knowledge is not a mere exterior knowledge, distanced from itself, subject to time, to the fact that, in time, something arrives, a datum or a series of data. On the contrary, it is knowledge that produces what it knows. By all accounts this sameness, the in-difference of the word and the name, could be guaranteed in no other way than by the self-given and founding name of God, name of all names. However, a distinction, a discrimination, a disjunction which distances the name must be at work *at the very heart* of the in-difference of the word and the name: otherwise man would be without language, without truly human language, he would not be man, for he would not have the ability to denominate which characterises him as a linguistic being.

Otherwise, then, God would be unable to complete his creation and would not be God. Creation is completed by a gift (*Gabe*). In completing his creation, God creates the human being in his own image, which means – according to Benjamin – that he does not create him with the word or on the basis of the word. God conceives man as different from nature by conceiving of his own being. Man has no *given* name. Of all the creatures, only man *gives* names and *gives himself* a name. The creation of man is a gift: a gift of the name, of language, *of the gift*. The gift of the name comes between two timelessnesses (between divine timelessness and the timelessness of paradise) to establish the 'paradisiacal language': 'In this second story of the Creation the making of man did not take place through the word: God spoke – and there was – but this man, who is not created from the word, is now invested with the *gift* (*Gabe*) of language and is elevated above nature.'[157] Man, an earthly creature, brought forth from the earth, from what is most natural, is nonetheless the other of nature and is so precisely because of his creation: he was not created by the word. What conclusion can be drawn from this interpretation of man's creation? Maybe what ensues is that the word moves outside of itself, that it does so at the very moment when the circle of divine sameness closes itself by allowing the name to be substituted for the word. The gift of the name (of the name which has not been given, of the name which can still be given and given again), this unique gift, which is consequently the only gift from God, implies the forgetting of the name. The name *is* the gift, it is always given, either by God or by man, even if only man can *give* things names since the thing named by its creator, by *the* creator, is not waiting for the name, it *is* the name; but as a gift, the name *is forgotten*. To give, to say *yes* to the other, is to forget; and to say *yes* to the gift received is to forget again. We could summarise what is said here by saying that forgetting is part of the 'apparition' of the name: for the 'apparition' does not let itself be thought separately from a thought of the gift, a thought which tries to take the gift as its starting point. It is *in* man – in language – that God gives language unto language, gives himself by forgetting himself: man is free because the ability to denominate which defines him – language, in other words – no longer stands in divine actuality and cannot actualise it except by reflecting it. Man's 'paradisiacal language' must already be a language of – pure and absolute – reflection:

> God did not create man from the word, and he did not name him. He did not wish to subject him to language, but in man God set language, which had served *Him* as medium of creation, free. God rested when he had left his creative power to itself in man. This creativity, relieved of its divine actuality, became knowledge (*Erkenntnis*). Man is the knower in the same language in which God is creator. Therefore the proposition that the spiritual essence of man is language needs explanation. His spiritual essence is the language in which creation took place. In the word creation took place, and God's linguistic essence is the word. All of human language is only reflection of the word in the name. The name is no closer to the word than knowledge to creation.[158]

The human act of denomination repeats and does not repeat the divine act: the name is preserved and separated by a non-repetitive repetition, by a repetition that cannot be repetitive. For denomination is the task assigned to man: his freedom is nothing more than assuming responsibility for this task. Man is the name as task:

> For God created things; the creative word in them is the germ of the cognising name, just as God, too, finally named each thing after it was created. But obviously this naming is only an expression of the identity of the creative word and

the cognising name in God, not the prior solution of the task that God expressly assigns to man himself: that of naming things.[159]

With the passage from God's language to man's paradisiacal language – the language of language – the name proper is separated from the word for the first time. Now the name can no longer be substituted for the word without a distance separating it; the name becomes the name of paradise – the first man names woman and things – and finally, after the 'Fall', it becomes the 'name in general' (*Name überhaupt*), always substituted, but for another name. The name appears. Which name happens to be closest to the name as the coincidence of name and word? The proper name, obviously. For the names given to things by mortals (could they give them proper names?) require a datum, the arrival of something which gives itself to be understood, through its incomprehensible language, as the thing that arrives. The proper name stands at the very frontier which divides the name, runs through language and marks the withdrawal and forgetting of the name.

> By giving names, parents dedicate their children to God; the names they give do not correspond – in a metaphysical, not etymological sense – to any knowledge, for they name newborn children. In a strict sense, no name ought (in its etymological meaning) to correspond to any person, for the proper name is the word of God in human sounds. By it each man is guaranteed his creation by God, and in this sense he is himself creative, as is expressed by mythological wisdom in the idea (which doubtless not infrequently comes true) that a man's name is his fate. The proper name is the communion of man with the *creative* word of God.[160]

Through the gift of the name, there is (are) generation(s). Philo of Alexandria writes: 'For this, he says, is "my name across the ages", inasmuch as it belongs to our time period, not to the precosmic, "and my memorial", not a name set beyond memory and thought, and again "for generations" (Exod. 3:15), not for beings ungenerated.'[161] But each generation, each new community, does nothing more than repeat the originary interruption or intermittence. For man's 'fate' is his name, and it is the name's 'fate' to make man forget the name as he gives it (again). 'The word for the being (*Wesen*) of the word is not granted', says Heidegger in his text on George's poem *Das Wort*.[162] The gift invariably includes forgetting, the movement out of oneself which doesn't wait for the 'Fall' and threatens to destabilise the internal economy of the Self – can we speak of a relation to oneself here? In the beginning was the word: so the 'Fall' is originary. The name is forgotten. This can be understood in two ways: (1) the name is forgotten because the bearer of a name who can give proper names and at the same time engender the body of the named never has the power to give himself the ability to denominate; (2) the name is forgotten because it is given thanks to God's forgetting ('God rested when he had left his creative power to itself in man'). *The name is forgotten because it is a gift.* The forgetting of the name is forgotten in the conventional theory of language. Isn't this theory 'conventional' inasmuch as it defines the name as the mark of a convention? For example, is the definition of the proper name given by Benveniste conventional or not? 'What we normally understand by the proper name is a conventional mark of social identification such that it can constantly and uniquely designate a unique individual.'[163] With the name, everything begins by not beginning, by beginning again without ever being able to begin. *There is no name without an apparition, but as soon as it appears, the name is no longer.* Is the *event*, here, as Benjamin affirms and must affirm, the 'Fall', the wounding of the name, the birth of abstract and juridical language which only parodies God's language? Must we not also say: the event is the gift of the name? Because of the forgetting of this event, because of the forgetting of the gift, which is not a mere accident, a *history* and *politics* become possible. For example – but it is the only example that can be given in this context – a 'politics' whose aim is its own negation, the negation of its name, a 'nihilistic politics', a politics which challenges all those who persistently attempt to establish universal laws. Benjamin, in the fragment called 'Theologico-political' – we do not know if he agreed to this title, since it is not on the manuscript, even though it is on the type-written copy – suggests that a 'world politics' should practise 'nihilism',[164] But it should not do so *in the name of* a negative teleology or a messianic tendency. 'History takes the place of names.'[165] Giorgio Agamben's remark fully captures Benjamin's thought. While agreeing with it, we could add that through the gift, the names have taken the place of the name. For what does Benjamin allow us to think? Maybe this: that all names keep a certain memory of the name, of the gift, because they are singular only in so far as they keep such a memory, a memory which keeps nothing, nothing but the given name which does not let itself be kept, which withdraws and is forgotten the moment it is given. What else would we keep but a name, your name, one's name? The 'logic' of the gift is an impossible 'logic': a gift which did not include forgetting would not be a gift. The giver must interrupt the relation to the other the very instant he establishes it by giving the gift. For this very reason, nothing prevents the gift from inscribing itself in an economy which transforms it. And it is surely on the condition that it becomes other that a gift can be received as such. But if forgetting were absolute, nothing would happen: a certain memory must bind the gift to the giver. This memory means that the gift is always a promise, something yet to come.[166] And in the space of this promise, in the space which separates us from the future, the gift again becomes other. The giver gives the gift, but he does not give the gift of giving oneself the gift; otherwise we would not experience the gift, the gift would be absolute and would erase itself immediately. The gift – of the name – is *unvordenklich*, it urges us to think the immemorial, it gives us the thought of the immemorial.[167]

The theologico-political

The name is given in its 'apparition'. There is no name without 'apparition' and no 'apparition' without a name. The 'apparition' has the same structure as the name. The name appears: it promises and causes a memory to emerge. It is there, in memory and promise, that we must situate the 'theologico-political'. I understand this term according to the meaning that Benjamin gave it. It describes the *contradictory* relation of two forces which attract each other. One makes the other stronger by moving away from it, the other draws the first towards it by withdrawing and letting it separate again. *Force* is the word

Benjamin uses. He compares the profane pursuit of happiness and the messianic tendency to two 'forces':

> If one arrow points to the goal toward which the profane dynamic acts, and another marks the direction of Messianic intensity, then certainly the quest of free humanity for happiness runs counter to the Messianic direction [the free man, who assumes the task of denomination, who names, strays and by straying approaches the name, A.G.D.]; but just as a force can, through acting, increase another that is acting in the opposite direction, so the order of the profane assists, through being profane, the coming of the Messianic Kingdom.[168]

Memory and promise, two words, it seems, to name two forces and perhaps also two languages: the language of the profane, of the historical, of the 'political' and the language of the 'theological', of the sacred, of messianic intensity. Clearly, and since the relationship between the two forces or languages is complex, we cannot simplify the matter by attributing memory to the 'political' and promise to the 'theological'. Memory already inscribes itself in the promise which, because of this, is other without being other: it is not otherwise. Unless it otherwise reinscribes itself in memory as promise. It is startling to point out the similarity between this structure of an 'intersecting without intersecting' and the structure that, for Heidegger, constitutes the relation of thought to *Dichten*. Perhaps we should not be too eager to underline the undeniable differences which separate the thought of Being from a 'theologico-political' thought. We could ask: what is the link which ties memory to promise in tying *Denken* to *Dichten*, in tying memory and promise to *Denken* and *Dichten*? The question is probably too general. However, it can produce very precise answers. I will restrict myself to quoting a passage from *L'Imitation des modernes*. After having reminded us of Heidegger's line which states that 'knowledge of history at its origin' (*Wissen von einer Ur-geschichte*) is a 'mythology', Philippe Lacoue-Labarthe writes:

> The project of a 'new mythology' has not ceased to haunt German thought. What is at stake here is certainly the possi-

bility of a national art [...] the possibility, for the Germans, of identifying themselves and existing as such. And so entering into history itself. The new mythology is the *promise* of history beginning (again).[169]

Is the promise involved in the relation between the profane quest for happiness and the messianic tendency due to a 'new mythology' which would try to create an original memory? No. The 'theologico-political' concept put forward by Benjamin is not the same as a 'mythology'. And if we wanted to denounce messianism as a 'myth' in the sense of the critique of religious ideologies, it would be a 'myth' without 'logos', a 'fiction' which breaks all alleged historical identifications and does not allow history to identify itself with itself, with an essence, a being proper to itself. Doesn't a certain critique of such ideologies spring from such an identification? What emerges from the passage quoted above is the difficulty of reaching the origin of history, for ever lost in the mists of time, *without* thinking of this origin as a *promise* – as a promise which is part of history or which strays from history at the beginning, thus exposing itself to forgetting. The aim of a 'new mythology' is precisely the return of a lost origin, still to come, its (re)appropriation. Does the immemorial origin, past and future, mark the place where memory and promise intersect to bind themselves together?

The 'theologico-political' promise does not simply ground historical unity: it destabilises it even as it grounds it, since the messianic tendency remains separate from the historical one.

Yet to come

Memory: always a promise of something to come. Promise: always a memory of something that has happened, has come to pass. And between the two, between memory and promise, man who names. In a text by Sholem on the different trends in Jewish messianism, we find an aphoristic line which summarises an important idea: 'Beginning at the moment of deepest catastrophe there exists the chance for redemption.'[171] This line seems to say that there is only the memory of the most terrible catastrophe to keep the promise of redemption. Its strange and disconcerting logic – we can tell what kind of political interpretations and justifications it could be used for – is a 'hyperbologic', to use a neologism from Lacoue-Labarthe. In the first chapter of his *Tractatus Theologico-Politicus*, Spinoza notes that 'a thing is referred to God' as an expression of 'the superlative degree, as in "the mountains of God", that is, very high mountains; "the sleep of God", that is, a very deep sleep'. It is in this sense, Spinoza adds, that 'we should explain Amos ch. 4 v. 11, where God himself says: "I have overthrown you as the overthrow of the Lord came upon Sodom and Gomorra." Divine overthrow is thus "*memorable* overthrow".'[172] A hyperbological superlative: the *more* memory is unable to comprehend the event, in other words: the more it is lacking (it only becomes necessary at that moment, at the moment of the deepest catastrophe), the *more* it is drawn towards its own foundation, towards a completely other event, promised to the chosen people and to the whole of mankind. This event stands behind all memory as its condition of possibility. The chance that Sholem speaks of is what arises when all is lost and cannot be regained: it is at the moment of the most terrible distress, when we have to find a memory and renounce it, that the possibility of a complete reversal appears. Another idea which does not seem alien to a thought of Being which evokes Hölderlin's poem dealing with danger (*Gefahr*) and rescue (*Rettung*). The promise is inscribed in memory. Inversely, the promise (of redemption) is only a promise inasmuch as it includes a memory (of the catastrophe). This is what Benjamin suggests in one of his theses on the concept of history: 'The Messiah comes not only as the redeemer, he comes as the subduer of the Antichrist. Only that historian will have the gift of fanning the spark of hope in the past who is firmly convinced that *even the dead* will not be safe from the enemy if he wins. And this enemy has not ceased to be victorious.'[173] If we give up memory, we forget the promise and sacrifice the dead. The sacrifice of the dead is the catastrophe which exceeds catastrophe, a catastrophe beyond catastrophe, with no possible turning back: it remains unthinkable for all thought. It is the unthinkable itself. All thought threatens to sacrifice the dead to the extent that we continue to think after the death of the other: which is always the case when we think. A promise demands from thought the impossible faithfulness of its memory. The historian Benjamin addresses does not speak in the name of the dead; he is only trying to guard the names in the face of the unthinkable – nothing is more difficult. A mortal being can never speak in the name of that which defines his condition and stops him from constituting himself as a subject which recognises itself in its own death. We are in danger of sacrificing the dead. Maybe the danger teaches us this: the impossibility of speaking in the name of death does not only prevent us from speaking *in the name of* a death of death, but also from speaking *in the name of* what is definitive, insurmountable, unsurpassable in death. Earlier, in a context determined by Rosenzweig's thought, we saw that the gift of the name is the other of a death that the name carries within itself. The promise is inscribed in memory and memory is inscribed in the promise. Memory and promise give themselves to be read in a double inscription: however, this inscription is not – yet – readable: 'Only the Messiah himself consummates all history, in the same sense that he alone redeems, completes, creates its relation to the Messianic. For this reason, nothing historical can relate itself on its own account to anything Messianic.'[174] Messianic history is written after the fact: as such, history is not messianic, even if history and messianism are not unrelated, not without a hyphen. This hyphen marks both an *alliance* and a *spacing*. The 'theologico-political' is the coming or the to-come of the Messiah: the 'theologico-political' exists only because the Messiah has not yet come. An absolute future, the absolute to come. When we speak of the future, the 'theologico-political' can always be involved even if no explicit reference to it is found. The future is reference itself, the reference of reference, reference without referent, because we cannot refer to the other to-come, at least as a finite, sensible, historical being. Benjamin is perfectly clear on this matter: 'nothing historical can relate itself on its own account to anything Messianic.' There is no *will to relate* in the 'theologico-political'. The future is the to-come of the other: the other comes against all expectations. A future (to come) which never lets itself be anticipated by a presence of any kind, but has already left a trace in the past.[175] This trace remains inappropriable: we cannot decide how the historical and the messianic, the 'theological' and the 'political', relate to each other. How can we then attribute a being, an essence, to the 'theologico-political'? The hyphen traverses the 'theological' and the 'political' and ties them to each other *before being*. The 'theologico-political' – in the sense that Benjamin seems to give or could give the term – is not a whole. Memory and promise are opposed to totalisation. Which can also be stated – but there is no alternative here – in the language of a thought of the name. The memory of the name, that is to say, its originary forgetting, is inseparable from the promise, from what the given name promises to knowledge: the gift itself. A name always promises another name, because it is given to be given, given again, and also refused. Isn't the Fall the refusal of the name? Memory and promise originate from the 'apparition' of the name. So the 'apparition' of the name which we must think of as both an interruption and an opening has the *structure of the hyphen* and, consequently, breaks down the totality which appropriates the names which are 'supposed to illustrate the stages of the concept in its movement'.[176]

Apparition – of art

'Apparition', the word 'apparition', appears frequently in Adorno's *Aesthetic Theory*. It appears in French: Adorno doesn't always translate it. 'Apparition' is already an apparition: 'apparition' as apparition, the memory and promise of a foreign language. It would have to be shown – I must forgo a detailed analysis here – that the sections on 'apparition' presuppose a reading of Benjamin, of what he writes about memory in the fifth of the 'Theses on the Philosophy of History'. There is nothing more fugitive than the 'apparition', Adorno states: it flees and takes what it would have allowed to be glimpsed with it. Or if it allows something to be glimpsed – but it is not a thing – it is because it becomes an image. Obviously, these elements of the economy of the 'apparition' are found in Benjamin: for him, the past is an apparition which has an illuminating effect the moment it appears and transforms itself into an image. The historiographer must retain this image that he cannot retain. If the past only comes to him through the image of its apparition, the apparition of the past is the ground of memory. But how can we describe the economy of the 'apparition' inas-

much as it is the 'apparition' of art? Works of art, according to
Adorno, are ciphered constellations of the other: what appears is
a 'non-being', it is the other, the 'apparition' *as* other. We
cannot formulate an economy of the 'apparition'. Its economy
is *catastrophic*. When he speaks of the 'apparition', Adorno is
thinking of the power of a catastrophe. He is thinking of the
power of an originary 'act' of violence which is repeated
endlessly:

> Artworks become appearances, in the pregnant sense of the
> term − that is, as the appearance of an other − when the
> accent falls on the unreality of their own reality. Artworks
> have the immanent character of being an act, even if they
> are carved in stone, and this endows them with the quality
> of being something momentary and sudden. This is regis-
> tered by the feeling of being overwhelmed when faced with
> an important work. [...] To this extent they are truly after-
> images (*Nachbilder*) of the primordial (*vorweltlich*) shudder.[177]

The 'apparition' forms and exceeds a work. We cannot think
the 'apparition' except on the grounds of excess and catastrophe.
Why? Because we will have already forgotten the other and we
will never have sufficiently forgotten. As soon as the catastrophe
occurs − at the beginning and *as* a beginning − an 'apocalyptic
tone' lets itself be heard: the catastrophe is both destructive and
revelatory. It could just as well be announcing the arrival of the
other as preventing him from arriving. As a sudden and unfore-
seen irruption, a catastrophic irruption, the 'apparition' surprises
and immobilises me: I feel as if I am being overwhelmed since
something appears and surprises me. To say that the 'apparition'
is an afterimage of the primordial shudder is to say that the
reaction it evokes involves a mechanism of identification or
assimilation. In *The Dialectic of Enlightenment*, Horkheimer and
Adorno call this mechanism a 'mimesis reflex'. It is a sort of
'apparition' (of the other), it is the 'apparition' itself which puts
the mechanism of identification or assimilation in place; the
word used by Horkheimer and Adorno is *Angleichung*. What is
the movement of this *mimesis*? Frozen by the irruption of the
other, which cannot be assimilated, exposed to a world without
world, *before* the world (*vorweltlich*), man likens himself to the

immobile nature which surrounds him. Here, nature is in fact
the other, the other that man experiences in the 'apparition'.
The 'mimesis reflex' is a type of self-conservation, self-constitu-
tion and self-affirmation, but it is *also* the sign of an opening.
There would be no relation to the other if we were not 'overwhelmed', if we were not surprised by the 'apparition'. The
economy of the apparition is aneconomic, it cannot be totalised.
The 'apparition' doesn't happen, it happens without happening:
to appear means to be transformed into an image, to imagine
(oneself). In other words, there are no pure 'apparitions', only
'images', *Bilder* and *Nachbilder* – but not *Abbilder*, imitations or
reproductions: 'Artworks are images as *apparitions*, as appearance
(*Erscheinungen*) and not as copy.'[178] Art is this imagination, this
imaginary essence of the 'apparition': the 'apparition' imagines
itself. It is a catastrophic imagination: 'Their *apparition*, which
makes artworks into images, always at the same time destroys
them as image (*Bildwesen*).'[179] Consequently, a work of art is
what remains of a work of art, of an image, of the nature of a
work of art as image, of the imagining and imagined 'apparition'.

We can see that Adorno tries to think *art* on the grounds of
the 'apparition': 'The appearance (*Aufgang*) of the nonexistant
as if it existed motivates the question as to the truth of art.'[180]
This sentence seems enigmatic, but it becomes a little more
intelligible – at least the first part – if we read the next
sentence: 'By its form alone art promises what is not; it regis-
ters objectively, however refractedly, the claim that because the
nonexistant appears it must indeed be possible.'[181] What exactly
do these two sentences mean? Doubtless one will be wary of
the philosophical language used, for the binary opposition
being/non-being seems to dominate the logic of the first
sentence. In the second sentence, which is also dominated by
this opposition, Adorno translates the 'appearing' of the 'apparition' by *erscheinen* and not, as we might have expected, by
aufgehen, the verb which corresponds to the substantive
Aufgang; to define *erscheinen*, he uses two pairs of concepts
which, like being/non-being, have dominated philosophical
thought in the West and determined its history; they are the
two pairs possibility/reality and subjectivity/objectivity.
However, I will not contest the use of this language; rather I

would like to draw attention to one particular point. It seems to me that the 'apparition' actually implies a strange obligation and that Adorno thinks of art as what I would call *the obligation of the 'theologico-political'*. But why art? Maybe because it holds the memory of the 'language of divine creation'[182] which Benjamin calls the 'language of things', or the 'language of names'. In any case, art is not an abstract language: it resists the abstraction of concretism as well as the abstraction of the concept: 'What appears is not interchangeable because it does not remain a dull particular for which other particulars could be substituted, nor is it an empty universal that equates everything specific that it comprehends by abstracting the common characteristics.'[183] Something appears, according to Adorno: *art*. It must be understood that every 'apparition' is an 'apparition' of art, in other words it is not an 'apparition' in a field which we assume is already formed and defined. Art is the trace of the 'apparition', the 'apparition' as trace: 'artworks from which the *apparition* has been driven out without a trace are nothing more than husks.'[184] How can we erase the trace of the 'apparition' and in that way erase the 'apparition' itself? How can we erase the trace of the name? Adorno leaves these questions unanswered. But we have noted that the 'apparition' has a relationship with the name, the gift of the name, the other. Its singularity is, in its structure, the singularity of the name. The other – this 'non-being' – comes to cipher itself (I am borrowing Adorno's term) into art, into the constellation of art. *Cipher*: an interruption which allows (nothing) to appear. The 'apparition' of art as the cipher of the other is the gift of a language which remains indecipherable even as it demands deciphering. Isn't this demand marked by the 'as if' (*als ob*)? Art appears. It has the form of a *promise* and calls for what it promises. The obligation to fulfil a promise is part of the act of promising itself. It may be impossible to keep a promise; but a promise without obligation would not be a promise. What does art promise? According to Adorno, it promises happiness. We are reminded of the importance Benjamin attaches to the 'pursuit of happiness': 'The order of the profane should be erected on the idea of happiness.'[185] A promise is essentially a 'promise of happiness'; happiness is part of the promise. Absolute despair would actually be the lack of promises. Which is the same as saying that the logic of the expression 'promise of happiness' that we find in Adorno's work is *self-inclusive*: to say that the promise is a 'promise of happiness' is to say that the promise promises happiness, but also that it promises yet another promise. The 'apparition' of art obliges us to remember another promise and the other as promise.

The chain of the will

This memory and promise are not rooted in will. As a *will to relate* – to the past or the future – will aims for its own reappropriation. By definition, it wants itself. According to Nietzsche, will is formed as a will to memory and is revealed in the promise, since the promise is the future of will, the future as will. Will without memory would be unable to promise and so would inevitably fail:

> And precisely this necessarily forgetful animal, in whom forgetting is a strength, representing a form of *robust* health, has bred for himself a counter-device, memory, with the help of which forgetfulness can be suspended in certain cases – namely in those cases where a promise is to be made: consequently it is by no means merely a passive inability to be rid of an impression once it has made its impact, nor is it just indigestion caused by giving your word on some occasion and finding you cannot cope, instead it is an active *desire* not to let go, a desire to keep on desiring what has been, on some occasion, desired, really it is the *will's memory*: so that a world of strange new things, circumstances and even acts of will may be placed quite safely in between the original 'I will', 'I shall do' and the actual discharge of the will, its *act*, without breaking this long chain of the will. But what a lot of preconditions there are for this! In order to have that degree of control over the future, man must first have learned to distinguish between what happens by accident and what by design, to think causally, to view the future as the present and anticipate it, to grasp with certainty what is end and what is means, in all, to be able to calculate, compute – and before he can do this, man himself will really have to become *reliable, regular, automatic [notwendig]*, even in his own

self-image, so that he, as someone making a promise is, is answerable for his own future!186

This is an excerpt from *On the Genealogy of Morality*. The promise is classed with the performative utterances; but what happens to this *act* if the 'chain of the will', the chain of 'acts of will' which link themselves together, is already broken? What happens to the act if it can't be an 'act of will'? My hypothesis is that memory and promise escape a thought which wants to secure both the past and the future of will, in other words will itself. For we cannot promise unless we expose ourselves, or even are already exposed, to finitude. A promise is, by definition, directed towards a finite being. We could say that we make promises to God – aren't vows like promises? Even so, it is a finite being who promises. The promise is always related to finitude. If the 'apparition' promises, it is because it marks a separation. All I am trying to do here is come closer to the 'gravity' which Jacques Derrida attributes to the promise. We could read the following lines as the opposite of Nietzsche; they are dedicated to Paul de Man:

A promise has meaning and gravity only with the death of the other. When the friend is no longer *there*, the promise is still not tenable, it will not have been made, but as a trace of the future it can still be *renewed*. You could call this an act of memory or a given word, even an act of faith; I prefer to take the risk of a singular and more equivocal word. I prefer to call this an *act*, only an act, quite simply an act.187

Catastrophic quotation – quoted catastrophe

What happens when a name – the name of a place, or rather: a non-place – comes to stand for the death of the other, but a death more terrible than death, this nameless death which forced Adorno to think the impossibility and necessity of thinking 'after Auschwitz'? What happens to the 'theologico-politi-cal' with the name 'Auschwitz'? Isn't extermination the catastrophe that Benjamin feared, the sacrifice of the dead? What mouth opens such that we fall into its abyss and are shattered whenever the name Auschwitz, the name of 'Auschwitz'

is pronounced? Doesn't this name which is not a name –
however, it is nothing else – signal (if it signals anything) the
irremediable, irreversible 'explosion' of the 'apparition', an explosion which does not set free anything that could still be considered to be revelatory? The explosion which Adorno calls
'apocalyptic'[188] *is* the 'apparition' itself. There would be no
'apparition' without blinding. The explosion, the catastrophe,
give the essence of the 'apparition' (... *eine Katastrophe, durch
die das Wesen des Erscheinens erst ganz freigelegt wird*).

I will quote a sentence of Adorno's. The sentence is already
read as a quote. Does anyone really read quotes? It is not necessary to expressly state that I am quoting, I don't need to say: I
will quote a line of Adorno's. The act marks itself. 'To write
poetry after Auschwitz is barbaric. And this corrodes even the
knowledge of why it has become impossible to write poetry
today.'[189] Can we quote this line, as I have just done? Maybe
we can quote this line of Adorno's only if we do *not* quote it
and only if we do *nothing* but quote it. Each time it is quoted, it
is betrayed. It is betrayed by the act of quoting, but also by the
refusal to quote. If I quote this line, I place it alongside other
lines, I turn it into an object of knowledge, a product of
thought, I make it the topic of a discussion, as if it could be
integrated into a theoretical discussion, as if it could be discussed
in the same way as other lines can. This line is unique and
singular, it cannot be repeated. I will always be compelled to
hear the imperative and categorical tone of this line, to hear it
as the enunciation of a *factum*, impossible to deduce, compelling
me before all obligation and beyond any quotation. But if I
refuse to quote it, I put it in danger of being forgotten, this line
which must not be forgotten, which says the necessity and
impossibility of remembering it. And my action also threatens
to isolate it and exclude it from discourse or thought, to make
others think it is a sort of holy name and that its singularity and
uniqueness mean that it cannot be linked with another line,
maybe even a question. My memory becomes forgetting.
Philippe Lacoue-Labarthe is rightly suspicious of the effect of
sanctification which is inseparable from the name, from
denomination.[190] However, the most fearsome consequence is
that by refusing to quote this line of Adorno's I deprive it of
the chance that all quotation entails. It is the chance of destruc-

tion: this, according to Benjamin, is the only chance of memory.

Can a name be quoted? The line quoted above is a name. Not because of any characteristic that we could say is representative of Adorno's thought and so would refer to his name, even if the line involved may contain a question that we could call *Adorno's* question. This line is part of a 'model' which bears the name of 'Auschwitz'. Jean-François Lyotard, following Adorno and using his concept of a 'model' (which is not a concept), has analysed the possibility of linking phrases or sentences to the name of 'Auschwitz', of *continuing to use language* after Auschwitz:

> As a model, 'Auschwitz' does not illustrate dialectics, be it negative. Negative dialectics blurs the figures of the concept, which proceed from the rule of the *Resultat*, and liberates the names that supposedly illustrate the stages of the concept in its movement. The idea of the model corresponds to this reversal in the destiny of dialectics: the model is the name for a kind of para-experience, where dialectics would encounter a non-negatable negative [*un négatif non niable*], and would abide in the impossibility of redoubling that negative into a 'result'.[191]

We know how many difficulties privileging *just one name* entails. One name, even this name, is never the only one to name evil. At the same time, the name, this name, will not allow any other name to be near it: any other name would violate the memory of the name, of this name which seems to constitute the very law of the name. The law of the name applies to this name much more than it applies to any other. It is the law of absolute singularity, of incommensurability, of that which is unparalleled. No name allows another name to be near it; all names are jealous and guard their privilege. For this reason, we cannot compare one name with another: as absolute singularity, each name forbids representation. To imagine the form of the name, as Adorno does, is perhaps inevitable; but it is already a transgression against the law. It is a necessary sacrilege, for otherwise there would be no name and no 'apparition'. The ban on representing or imagining, the prohibition of images (*Bilderverbot*), this 'theologico-political' motif which is omnipresent in Adorno's thought, refers to the importance attached to the name. 'Auschwitz' is the name of that which bears no relation to other names, of what remains unnameable and conceals itself from imagination. 'Auschwitz' is 'nameless'. But what Jewish thought reveals about the name is that the name hides itself and that its law is the law of withdrawal, reservation, of the crypt. The name encrypts (itself). Absolute singularity escapes (itself). In his work 'The Name of God According to a Few Talmudic Texts', Levinas writes: 'But the proper name, close to what is named, is not connected logically with it; consequently, despite this proximity, it is an empty shell like a permanent revocation of what it evokes, a disembodiment of what is embodied through it. Through being forbidden to be uttered, it is held between the two: a Tetragrammaton that is never pronounced in the way it is written.' The passage from 'Thou' (denomination makes it possible to address someone in this way) to 'He' (a form of address that highlights the gap and the separation) is essential to the name: 'Thou becomes He in the name, as if the name belonged simultaneously to the upright straightforwardness of being addressed as Thou and to the absolute of holiness.'[192] The name blocks the path which it clears: this is its law, the law itself, as we will see.

Benjamin states that the law is established, that it establishes itself at the moment of the Fall: we fall under the influence of the law in post-'Adamite' language. But the law draws man to it, it seduces him, it says to him: come. 'This judging word expels the first human beings from paradise; they themselves have aroused it in accordance with the *immutable law* by which this judging word punishes – *and expects* – its own awakening as the only, the deepest guilt. In the fall, since the eternal purity of names was violated, the sterner purity of the judging word arose.'[193] The purity of judgement doubles the purity of the name: from this moment, the name makes the law and judges. We can fall under the influence of the law because we forget, we forget ourselves: forgetting is the law's condition of possibility. As soon as language is given, as soon as the name is forgotten, that is to say *before* the Fall, the voice of the law starts to seduce man, who was created by forgetting – by God's forgetting. It is as if the law requires forgetting and forgetting was the law, programmed by a law older than the law, an 'eternal' law, the law of the awakening of the law or the law as the law of the awakening of the law. The name, the withdrawal of which makes the law, says: come, stand before me, keep me. And at the same time, as it withdraws, it says: go away, forget me, betray me. Which translates into: come, keep me still, do not forget me, etc.

'Auschwitz', the name of God: obligations

If the singularity of the name of God consists in the absolute revoking of what it evokes, if it evokes only by revoking and revokes only by evoking, a hypothesis can be risked. I say 'risked' because it seems to me that this hypothesis could be rejected on very serious grounds: it demands a certain imprudence and violence, even irresponsibility. Despite all that must be said about the name as such and its law – and not by simple analogy – only the name of 'Auschwitz' is able to make the law made by the name of God.[194] But we must speak the name of 'Auschwitz', it must not be replaced. That which is beyond comparison, which evokes absolutely, must be named. This is the imperative of the name: 'A new categorical imperative has been imposed by Hitler upon unfree mankind: to think and act in such a way that Auschwitz will not repeat itself, and that nothing similar will happen. When we want to find reasons for it, this imperative is as refractory as the given one of Kant was once upon a time. Dealing discursively with it would be an outrage.'[195] Hitler imposed a new categorical imperative on men, an imperative of the name: act and think in such a way that Auschwitz is never repeated and nothing similar happens; which is to say: act and think as if Auschwitz could happen again, as if it had *already* happened several times. (If Auschwitz happens only once, it is because this name points to an event which will never stop happening.) We cannot deduce Adorno's imperative, we cannot think it by means of discursive thought, we cannot think it with the thought of the transcendental: for the confusion of transcendental and historical or empirical levels is not an error of thought at all. This is precisely what 'Auschwitz', this name which from now precedes all thought, makes us think. Can we speak of a new categorical imperative? Can we speak of a *sacrilege* if we attempt to deduce it? Can we impose a categorical imperative on the categorical imperative? Can a name do so? These questions intersect in this question: why continue to speak of a 'categorical imperative' after Auschwitz?

It seems that there is a relation between the obligation imposed by the name and that of the – moral – law. The name which must not be uttered forbids representation.

Perhaps there is no more sublime passage in the Jewish law than the commandment: Thou shalt not make unto thee any graven image (*Bildnis*), or any likeness (*Gleichnis*) of any thing that is in heaven or on earth, or under the earth, etc. This commandment can alone explain the enthusiasm which the Jewish people, in their moral period (*gesittete Epoche*), felt for their religion when comparing themselves with others, or the pride inspired by Mohamedanism. The very same holds good of our representation of the moral law and of our native capacity for morality. The fear that, if we divest this representation of everything that can commend it to the senses, it will thereupon be attended only with a cold and lifeless approbation and not with any moving force or emotion, is wholly unwarranted. The very reverse is the truth. For when nothing any longer meets the eye of sense, and the unmistakable and ineffaceable idea of morality is left in possession of the field (*unverkennbare und unauslöschliche Idee*), there would be need rather of tempering the ardour of an unbounded imagination to prevent it rising to enthusiasm, than of seeking to lend these ideas the aid of images and childish devices for fear of their being wanting in potency.[196]

We stand before the name as we stand before the law. The name conceals itself and gives itself to be read. So, the name's double-bind is the law's double-bind. We must expose ourselves to the absence of the name and endure being-exposed. We endure something when we cannot stay upright because we have no support and because we must stay in the double-bind. Such an 'attitude' is not necessarily, as we might think, the sign of a lack of faith. But it is always a dangerous political 'attitude'. Kant continues: 'For this reason governments have gladly let religion be fully equipped with these accessories, seeking in this way to relieve their subjects (*Untertan*) of the exertion, but to deprive them, at the same time, of the ability (*Vermögen*), required for expanding their spiritual powers (*Seelenkräfte*) beyond the limits arbitrarily laid down for them, and which facilitate their being treated as though they were merely passive.'[197] The name conceals itself and allows other names – the names of the name – to replace it, to substitute themselves for it. In the first volume of his autobiography, Juan Goytisolo evokes the figure of Benjamin at the moment when he first crosses the Spanish-French border. But he does not name Benjamin. As if *respect* forbade naming this name. As if this frontier carried Benjamin's name. As if the name of the one who does not name substituted itself for the name of the other. Minimalisation and monumentalisation of the name: does my name become more powerful by substituting for the name of the other? Does the name of the other become more powerful by allowing my name to be substituted for it? By concealing itself, the name forces man to remember. The name's retreat reminds man of his finitude, the fact that he is unable to speak the word. Because he can neither create nor name as God does, man can only enter into relation with the name through the names of the name. He needs another name. The name keeps man at a distance from the name; like the law, it postpones their meeting. This is its fatality. For the name which turns man away from the name can turn him towards memory *and* towards forgetting. Kant makes it clear that it requires a certain productivity of the imagination for the law which forbids representation to be obeyed. The law cannot contain the productive and independent imagination, overflowing and unlimited, unless it negotiates with it: imagination must be productive when the government tries to limit autonomy; but it must limit itself so that the law is not transgressed. A certain enthusiasm fired by the imagination can be seen as the sign of a civilised era with a moral conscience ('The idea of the good linked to affectivity is called enthusiasm'); but imagination is in danger of turning the enthusiasm it arouses into exaltation, into daydreaming, into fanaticism (*Schwärmerei*) if it does not submit to its own restrictions. The relationship with the name is always complex. The name forces us to expose ourselves to its absence, to endure this being-exposed and to enter into a relationship with the names of the name. Its law is the law:

> For the law is the forbidden, a terrifying double-bind in its own operation. It is the forbidden: this does not mean that it forbids, but that it is itself forbidden, a forbidden place. It interdicts and contradicts itself by placing the man in his own contradiction: one cannot reach the law, and in order to have a rapport of respect with it, *one must not* — *one must not* have a rapport to the law but *must disrupt the relation.* One must *enter into relation* with the law's representatives, its examples, its guardians. And these are the interrupters as well as the messengers.[119]

'Auschwitz' is a terrible name, the most terrible name, more terrible than any other name, because it cannot be sublime: it erases the ineffaceable (*unauslöschlich*) idea of morality spoken of by Kant. Its memory is one *without any idea.* This makes it all the more compelling: its obligation is *beyond* the idea of morality and its obligation. This may be what thought can no longer think. How could we think otherwise? 'Auschwitz' is incommensurable: not only because *nothing similar* can be thought or imagined but above all because something unlike anything else compels us to think and act in such a way that *nothing similar* ever happens. If Adorno has a question, if Adorno's question is that of the name, I think that it 'presents' itself in this formless form.

Exclusion

> There will be no poetry after Auschwitz,
> unless it is on the grounds of Auschwitz.
> (Peter Szondi)[199]

Can we keep a name? The name obliges us to be faithful: we must keep the name which conceals itself in order to keep thought from ideology. An ideological proposition could be one of the form: 'Auschwitz' is nothing more than a name among names and can be replaced by any other name. The name warns us. Adorno and Horkheimer stress this function of

the name: 'In Jewish religion, in which the idea of the patriarch-
ate culminates in the destruction of myth, the bond between
name and being is still recognised in the ban on pronouncing
the name of God [...] Jewish religion allows no word that
would alleviate the despair of all that is mortal (*Verzweiflung
alles Sterblichen*). It associates hope only with the prohibition
against calling on what is false as God, against invoking the
finite as the infinite, lies as truth.'[200] Not giving a name, which
means not giving several names to what has only one name,
what is unique – this is a motif which Cohen also insists upon
when he says that the name of the Jewish God does not play the
role of a magical instrument (*Zaubermittel*), since it is actually
monotheism, the uniqueness of the name, which protects it
from magic (*Zauberei*).[201] But to simply oppose multiplicity –
the magical or ideological use of names – to unity – the non-
magical use or non-use of names – and a regressive obscurant-
ism to a progressive enlightenment, remains an extremely
problematic gesture. Freud, for example, notes an irreducible
continuity which ties magic to spiritual progress:

> In our children, in adult neurotics as well as in primitive
> people, we find the mental phenomenon which we have
> called the belief in the 'omnipotence of thoughts'. We judge
> it to be an over-estimation of the influence which our mental
> faculties – the intellectual ones in this case – can exert on the
> outer world by changing it. All magic, the predecessor of
> science, is basically founded on these premises. All magic of
> words belongs here, as does the conviction of the power con-
> nected with the knowledge and the pronouncing of the
> name. We surmise that the 'omnipotence of thoughts' was
> the expression of the pride mankind took in the development
> of language, which had brought in its train such an extraor-
> dinary increase in the intellectual faculties. There opened
> then the new realm of spirituality where conceptions, mem-
> ories and deductions became of decisive importance, in con-
> trast to the lower psychical activity which concerned itself
> with the immediate perceptions of the sense organs. It was
> certainly one of the most important stages on the way to
> becoming human [...] The progress in spirituality consists
> in deciding against the direct sense perception in favour of

the so-called higher intellectual processes, that is to say, in favour of memories, reflection and deduction. An example of this would be the decision that paternity is more important than maternity, although the former cannot be proved by the senses as the latter can. This is why the child has to have the father's name and inherit after him. Another example would be: our God is the greatest and mightiest, although He is invisible like the storm and the soul.[202]

When we place too much trust in the operation which opposes a monotheistic enlightenment to a pagan counter-enlightenment, there is a risk of confusing what we want to avoid confusing at all costs. To refuse giving a name, to refuse identifying name and knowledge: the one who names, who addresses the other by naming him, affirms a relation which cannot be reduced to knowledge without therefore being simply magical or mystic. The name marks a limit of knowledge. The limit marked by the name 'Auschwitz' is one which forbids knowledge itself. The historian, according to Lyotard, cannot do without this name:

> But then, the historian must break with the monopoly over history granted to the cognitive regimen of phrases, and he or she must venture forth by lending his or her ear to what is not presentable under the rules of knowledge. Every reality entails this exigency insofar as it entails possible unknown senses. Auschwitz is the most real of realities in this respect. Its name marks the confines wherein historical knowledge sees its competence impugned. It does not follow from that that one falls into non-sense. The alternative is not: either the meaning that science establishes, or absurdity, be it of the mystical kind.[203]

If the name obliges us to be faithful, it also obliges us to be unfaithful, to betray it. In the debate around the linguistic, ethical and philosophical relevance which should be attributed to the name of 'Auschwitz', Jacques Derrida warns us against discourses which, taking Auschwitz as a model,

> are in danger of reconstituting a sort of centrality, a 'we' which is certainly not that of speculative dialectics but which

is related to the unanimous privilege which we occidental Europeans accord to Auschwitz in the fight or the question which we oppose to speculative dialectics, to a certain type of occidental reason. The danger is that this 'we' would take from memory or sideline proper names other than Auschwitz, ones which are just as abominable, names which have names and names which have no name.[204]

The name reproduces the violence it produces when naming. A name always wants to be the only one to name what it names, that is its narcissism, narcissism itself. Isn't narcissism necessarily tied to the name? We must link on to the name, we must speak of 'Auschwitz' after Auschwitz, for instance by keeping to the rules of historical knowledge. We must take the power of exclusion, the *exclusivity*, from the name. The violence of the name which sidelines other names demands that we are violent towards it and distance ourselves from it. In the name, inside the name, we become blind, we see only the name, we see nothing. We find ourselves in absolute exteriority. Adorno writes: 'How one should think instead has its distant and vague prototype in the various languages, in the names which do not categorically cover the thing, albeit at the cost of the cognitive function of language. In undiminished cognition we want what we have been drilled to renounce, what the names that come too close will blind us to – resignation and delusion are ideological complements.'[205] So the name is at once prototype and simulacrum, the prototype of the simulacrum and the simulacrum of the prototype, it is the inextricable interlacing of the prototype and the simulacrum – of thought. Its power of exclusion is due to the blinding proximity that keeps the letter safe from man by making it unreadable. But the simulacrum itself is only a sort of prototype: the prototype of a freedom necessary for thought. In 1930 Adorno notes:

The lines of our destiny cross each other and form an inextricable interlacing. Names are the seals which, time and again, put their mark on the drawing of the lines. By showing us initials that we do not understand, but which we follow, they protect the lines in such a way that we cannot take hold of them; but as they hold us, they stop us from entangling ourselves, taken by the criss-crossing lines.[206]

Names free us from destiny even as they deliver us unto that which is beyond our calculations.

When I quoted the sentence from Adorno, I asked: what kind of sentence are we dealing with? And I tried to reply, perhaps too elliptically: like the name that it names, this sentence is a name, an 'apparition', the irremediable explosion of the 'apparition'. It is a name, the name of a model, because it is absolutely singular, because its singularity is the singularity of the name. Thought cannot do otherwise than to think on the grounds of this sentence, this name. It is impossible to return to a past or to refer to a future which has not already been determined by Adorno's sentence or line. It cannot be lifted or limited, even if it is necessary to ask questions about it. It does not illustrate thought. We know that Adorno once quoted it to say the opposite of what it says:[207] 'Perennial suffering has as much right to expression as a tortured man has to scream; hence it may have been wrong to say that after Auschwitz one could no longer write poems.' But we cannot use this other sentence to justify 'poetry' or legitimise thought. The two sentences are contradictory statements *and yet they do not contradict each other.* The second sentence, from the text 'After Auschwitz', the title of a 'meditation on metaphysics', is not just a revocation. It does not simply limit the power of the first sentence, even if the former somehow called for the latter. *The relationship between them is irreducibly asymmetric.* They are two sentences, two names beyond exclusion. All reading must take into account the incommensurable relationship between these two sentences. 'But it is not wrong to raise the less cultural question whether after Auschwitz you can go on living – especially whether one who escaped by accident, one who by rights should have been killed, may go on living. His mere survival calls for the coldness, the basic principle of bourgeois subjectivity, without which there could have been no Auschwitz; this is the drastic guilt of him who was spared.'[208]

In an essay on poetry and society, Adorno speaks of a 'lyrical language' (*lyrisches Wort*): 'Only by virtue of a differentiation taken so far that it can no longer bear its own difference; only

by virtue of a differentiation that cannot tolerate anything but
the universal in the particular, the universal freed from the
humiliation of an isolation or a mere specification (*Vereinze-
lung*), does lyrical language represent language's intrinsic being
as opposed to its service in the realm of ends.'[209] 'Lyrical
language' is then a difference, a singular language or speech, it is
the difference or the singularity of speech in language. Nothing
forces us to think that this singularity is always that of a poem.
But maybe all (lyrical?) poems are traversed by it. The singularity we are dealing with here is not the result of a differentiation
or individualisation of the universal. The relation between the
singular and the universal must be thought differently. Isn't
what Adorno calls the 'universal' (*das Allgemeine*) above all
language, language as such or language in general? Speech is
singular – and lyrical – where the universal becomes singular
and singularity becomes universal. But this becoming does not
in any way have the meaning of what we currently call specification. All specification already assumes that the universal is
dominant. The singularity of lyrical language or speech, by
contrast, never presupposes anything. It is a singularity without
singularity, it is a difference because it is not a difference,
because it is not opposed to the universal. Language is lyrical
inasmuch as its essence draws on a singularity without singularity, a singularity without opposition. For as a singularity
without singularity, speech stands in for language, for something which is essential to it and cannot be reduced to its prag-
matic use. The singular immediately exposes itself to the
universal, beyond positivity and negativity; this immediacy is
no longer opposed to mediation. The singular and the universal,
speech and language come to pass in their exposition or as an
exposition which does not turn into a position. The exposure of
speech to language constitutes its singularity. This, of course,
does not mean that it is something determined, since the possibility of determination already implies the predominance of the
universal. What if 'lyrical language' were *free* speech? Doesn't
Adorno point to this freedom when he writes that as it stands in
for language, lyrical language also stands in for a 'free humanity'? Is the impossibility of writing a poem after Auschwitz –
statement and interdiction, both at once – the impossibility of
achieving free speech, of experiencing such speech? But there

would be neither a statement nor an interdiction if thought which is directly concerned with the impossibility of writing a poem could not gesture towards freedom. Isn't Auschwitz precisely what constrains us to think another freedom? From the start, the sentence 'We can no longer write poetry after Auschwitz' is strictly unthinkable, without relation to thought, if it remains isolated. Adorno could not write this sentence without writing the one he wrote fifteen years later ('We have the right to write poetry after Auschwitz'). However, he could not establish a simple symmetry between the two either. In 1962 Adorno returns – for the first time?[210] – to his first sentence. He has not yet written the second sentence. In this third passage, the second according to a chronological order, Adorno states the following:

> I do not want to soften my statement that it is barbaric to continue to write poetry after Auschwitz; it expresses, negatively, the impulse that animates committed literature [...] But Hans Magnus Enzensberger's rejoinder also remains true, namely that literature must resist precisely this verdict, that is, be such that it does not surrender to cynicism merely by existing after Auschwitz. It is the situation of literature itself and not simply one's relation to it that is paradoxical.[211]

So, by holding to the chronological order (1951–1962–1966) we could claim that Adorno has passed from an affirmation to a revocation and that the passage cited above is that very passage: the construction of a paradox – affirmation and revocation – in the *interval* between an affirmation and a (quasi)-revocation. We would then be relying on a continuity of reflection. Even if it is not wrong to do so, we would not be grasping the essential, what makes Adorno's thought singular. The first sentence (1951) is unthinkable without the second (1966), but the latter remains unthinkable without the former: the second sentence never stops clashing with the first. The *gravity* of these two lines is that of the name of 'Auschwitz', divided even as it remains indivisible. It stems from this dissymmetry, this contradiction without contradiction. And it is this gravity which affects the very idea of a continuity of reflection. To propose such a conti nuity means reducing 'Auschwitz' and – at the extreme –

making it a stage of the dialectic, a negative that can ultimately be negated.

We read the sentence which states the impossibility of writing a poem after Auschwitz – what is a poem? what is it to write a poem? – as we would read a quote: I have already laid great stress upon this. But I would like to point out again what seems most decisive: 'as a quote' does not just mean that it is a 'hackneyed' phrase, that it is too 'hackneyed', that we quote it without really thinking about what it means and sometimes just to produce a specific effect. Isn't this effect already programmed by the sentence, by its banality, by the 'immense and unbearable banality' of the 'after-Auschwitz', by the necessity which this name imposes, or better, by the necessity that the sentence imposes by imposing this name?[212] If we read this sentence as we read a quote, it is because we almost never read the whole sentence, in its entirety. We only read the first part: we forget half the sentence in the same way that we forget what is not quoted in the quote, the context or the omitted words: 'To write poetry after Auschwitz is barbaric. *And* this corrodes even the knowledge (*Erkenntnis*) of why it has become impossible to write poetry today.' The sentence which states the impossibility of writing a poem after Auschwitz states the impossibility of *thinking* after Auschwitz.

Thinking against thought

After Auschwitz, the meditations on metaphysics (the meditations that bear this title and those we find in all of Adorno's works) point to the confrontation of thought and death. Referring to the analyses of the philosopher Alfred Schmidt,[213] we could say that the concept of *materialism*, which Adorno uses frequently, is a 'limit-concept' of thought, a concept which stands at the edge of meaning and, for this reason, is no longer subject to the law of the concept. If the 'absence of images' (*Bilderlosigkeit*) in Adorno's materialism[214] and the *Bilderverbot* converge, it is also and most of all because of finitude: 'Materialism', Adorno states, 'is the philosophy that would bring death into consciousness without reducing or sublimating it.'[215] What does it mean to 'bring death into consciousness' without sublimating it, without idealising it, without imagining it? Is it possible? The 'consciousness' of which Adorno speaks cannot be the awareness of oneself conceived of by metaphysical thought: this consciousness must be defined in another way. How? Not on the basis of subjective self-representation, of the experience and certitude of the subject, but maybe on the basis of the vigilant memory of a thought which would think *against* thought, against a thought which would want to turn in upon itself, against the thought of thought as the thought of identity. The fact of thinking after the death of the other which cannot be thought: nothing else, Adorno seems to suggest, should be thought. Thinking about thinking is thinking *against* thinking, since thought never stops mastering death by sublating it, by thinking a dialectical death of death. Against this death of death, against the idealisation of death, Adorno sets another death of death, a death of death more terrible than death. It destabilises the established opposition between life and death: 'Since Auschwitz, fearing death means fearing worse than death.'[216] The survivor of Auschwitz can neither live nor die, he survives death as a passage from natural life to the 'ideal life of consciousness':

> The guilt of a life which purely as a fact will strangle other life, according to statistics that eke out an overwhelming number of killed with a minimal number of rescued, as if this were provided in the theory of probabilities – this guilt is irreconcilable with living. And the guilt does not cease to reproduce itself, because not for an instant can it be made fully, presently conscious. This, nothing else, is what compels us to philosophise.[217]

In an essay called 'After the Fact' and *after* having named Adorno, Blanchot writes:

> The need to bear witness is the obligation of a testimony that can only be given – and given only in the singularity of each person – by the impossible witnesses – the witnesses of the impossible [one is reminded here of Horkheimer's phrasing in the passage cited above, A.G.D.]; some have survived, but their survival is no longer life, it is the break from living affirmation, the attestation that the good that is life (not nar-

cissistic life, but life for others) has undergone the decisive blow that leaves nothing intact.

A few lines on, we find a sentence which reminds us strangely of Rosenzweig's thought, as if this sentence was reproducing the constraints of the privilege accorded to eternal life at the very moment where this privilege is no longer a privilege and the sentence itself comes into conflict with it. *It remains the only privilege*, this time the privilege of drawing all privileges into irreversible loss. Sur-viving – sur-vival which sur-vives the sur-vival of the name, but also the sur-vival of the only name which describes the 'after' – henceforth means: dying more than once. We can no longer die and we can do nothing other than die: 'Humanity as a whole had to die through the trial of some of its members (those who incarnate life itself, almost an entire people, a people that has been promised an eternal presence). This death still endures. And from this comes the obligation never again to die only once, without however allowing repetition to inure us to the always essential ending.'[218]It is as if something had been left intact: a certain privilege which translates into a certain sur-vival which sur-vives sur-vival.

How do we name a thought that thinks against thought? Adorno speaks of 'philosophical' thought, maybe because he attaches a truthfulness to it that we need not press ourselves to denounce: 'If negative dialectics calls for the self-reflection of thinking, the tangible implication is that if thinking is to be true – if it is to be true today in any case – it must also be a thinking against itself.'[219] The word we could use to name this thought belongs to Heidegger's lexicon: it plays a very important part in the essays he wrote as he read and re-read Hölderlin. It is therefore a German word: the word *Andenken*. *Andenken* is memory, the fact that we remember something, something which will return and belongs to the future (Heidegger insists on this in the lectures on Hölderlin's poetry).[220] But the word also indicates that we approach something which does not let itself be approached, which offers a certain resistance to thought: *An-denken*. *Andenken* tries to approach everything that resists it, or, more exactly, it tries to let itself be approached by the other who is to come so that it can keep him by forgetting him and make sure that he will return. There is *Andenken* because thought implies forgetting the other, a reduction of its alterity, an identification of the 'non-identical', a reification or mortification: 'If each of the dead resembles one who was murdered by the living, that person is also like one they ought to have rescued.'[221] We seem to be able to find in this line of Adorno's the terrifying idea of a sacrifice of the dead. To keep and guard the dead in order to prevent them from being sacrificed and in this way rescue them, rescue them without *'making death work'*[222] – that is what the work of the thought of *Andenken* would consist of. But how can we keep the dead, the other who is mortified by thought? Thought abandons the other, it delivers him unto forgetting, it leaves that which it tried to think or to rescue to die, that which, suddenly, returns, returns as something else: 'Nothing can be rescued unchanged, nothing that has not passed through the portal or the gateway (*Tor*) of its death.'[223] It would be easy to class this phrase among the utterances of speculative dialectics – or, if we follow the use of the verb 'to rescue', to show that it designates the idea of the resurrection of the dead on the final day of judgement. We cannot argue with such interpretations. But what we must also do is attempt to decipher the constellations of Adorno's thought starting from the *name*. I would say, deciphering the 'apparition' of the name even further, that the 'gateway of death' (*Tor des Todes*) *is* the name, the name that is as 'dark as a gateway'. If the name is too close to the named, as Adorno suggests, it is because it freezes or paralyses it and thus takes it towards nothingness, towards the limit of language. If we come too close to the name, we are in danger of being paralysed. We must always mourn what is named. For the name *already* identifies the thing, as Jacques Derrida stresses:

> The thing: magnificent and classed, at once raised above all taxonomy, all nomenclature, and already identifiable in an order. To give a name is always, like any birth (certificate), to sublimate a singularity and to inform against it, to hand it over to the police. All the police forces in the world can be routed by a surname, but even before they know it, a secret computer, at the moment of baptism, will have kept them up to date.[224]

However, something eludes this computer: the identification of the thing by the name necessarily forgets that it was a gift. Denomination is an 'over-naming' and is so because of the straying of the name, because of its separation, because of the originary interruption. There are never enough and always too many names. A name names more than it names. In other words: what is named can haunt the name, make it turn and return, for example, under another name. This is the whirl of the name. There is no identity of the name, or of the named, or of the name and the named.

Als ob

Because it names more than it names, the name is a promise. But as soon as denomination is over-naming, the name – what appears, always art, its singularity – becomes inseparable from the constellation: 'By their negativity, even as total negation, artworks make a promise, just as the gesture (*Gestus*) with which narratives once began or the initial sound struck on a sitar promised what had never been heard *before*, never been seen, even if it was the most fearsome.'[225] The work of art, the constellation as 'apparition', is a promise. It is a name. And the poem, in its very singularity, its given singularity, is the name *par excellence*. Is writing a poem after Auschwitz barbaric because all poems are promises, because a poem still promises, even if it promises what is most fearsome? No poem after Auschwitz means: after Auschwitz there can be no more promises, or names, 'Auschwitz confirmed the philosopheme of pure identity as death.'[226]

Nonetheless, we have to testify – and there can be no testimony without names. Is testimony already a sign of hope? How can we think hope? Does it consist in the uncertainty of the call, in the not-knowing that all promises entail, in the exposure to the call of a promise? Hope is past or to come, it escapes the one who tries to keep it – until death:

> For the gaze [...] which leaves it behind, the earth is rounded to a sphere that can be overviewed, it appears as in the pictures which in the meantime have been taken from space, not the centre of Creation but something minute and

ephemeral. To such experience is allied the melancholy hope for other stars, inhabited by happier beings than humans. But the earth that has grown remote to itself is without the hope the stars once promised. It is shrinking into empty galaxies. On it lies beauty as the reflection of past hope, which fills the dying eye until it is frozen below the flakes of unbound space.[227]

Thought as *Andenken* is inseparable from the name and the promise, from the name *as* promise. The name is a promise, because it keeps man at a distance, because it is the 'unique phenomenon of a distance':[228]

What is a metaphysical experience? If we disdain projecting it upon allegedly primal religious experiences, we are most likely to visualise it as Proust did, in the happiness, for instance, that is promised by village names like Otterbach, Watterbach, Reuenthal, Monbrunn. One thinks that going there would mean entering the fulfilled, as if it existed. Being really there makes the promise recede like a rainbow. And yet one is not disappointed; the feeling now is one of being too close, rather, and not seeing it for that reason.[229]

When he defines the name and establishes a relationship between the name and the promise, between a blinding proximity and an illuminating distance, Adorno uses the formula which defines the 'apparition' of art: 'as if it existed' (*als ob es wäre*). If we wanted to show that a thought is poetic – as Hannah Arendt wishes to say of Benjamin[230] – we should necessarily refer to the name and the formula of the 'apparition'. What does Adorno say about the promise? He says this: a promise cannot be kept, but this impossibility does not imply any disappointment. A promise is not a mere anticipation. I cannot make a promise unless it is impossible for me to anticipate the effects of that promise. If I know in advance what is going to happen, well then, in this case the promise is not a promise. A promise is excessive: there always has to be another promise to the promise, another name for the name which promises, promises itself in promising a certain happiness. The disappointment[231] may be the symptom of a confusion: we confuse the promise and what is promised. We can't endure the fact that the name withdraws. This does not mean that we can promise absolutely anything: a promise must be kept. The name as promise forces us to promise to remember it, to keep it in our memory. But remembering demands the possibility of forgetting. What does the name promise? As the prototype of thought in language, it promises a certain experience of language, an experience of language as gift: it promises a name and another name, a promise and another promise, another 'apparition' of the name as promise. As soon as there is a promise, there are others; there is never only one promise, that is what makes the happiness of all promises, what makes every promise a promise of happiness. *Andenken*: the memory of the coming of the name, a memory which does not hold meaning but an inscription that all names carry: *there are names*, and there are *also* inadmissible names, absolutely singular names which destroy singularity, for example, what we call the 'singularity of the poem', names which oblige even more, beyond obligation.

The name and Being

Heidegger speaks of the promise of Being in his lectures on 'Nihilism as determined by the history of Being':

> Addressing in this way, while withholding itself in default, *Being is the promise of itself.* To think in order to encounter Being itself in its default means to become aware of the promise, as which promise Being itself 'is'. It is, however, in staying away; that is to say, insofar as there is nothing to it.[232]

Being is nothing, it conceals itself, it is a promise inasmuch as it conceals itself, and it is nothing. But we cannot keep Being and remain attentive to its promise except by giving names and keeping the given name. *Was heißt Denken?* is clear on this point: Being or that which gives Being obliges (*heißt*) us to name so that something can appear. Every time a name is given, there is a promise and a promise of the promise (*Verheißung*: an announcement which promises). Certainly

Being is not a name; but it is not the other of the name either, it is the name, the name of the name. Being is before the name, it is earlier. There is nothing before the name, only Being, that which gives both Being and the name, the originary call, the call which is a gift, the gift of denomination. As Heidegger says in his essay on George: the word of the word, the name of the name is lacking, because this word, this name, is nothing, it is not a word, it is not a name, it gives the word, it gives the name, it is not simply the other of the word, the other of the name, it is the word, it is the name, other. The name is (not) nothing. Nothing is more difficult than giving a name, nothing is more difficult than naming things by their names. Heidegger experienced this by naming and refusing to name. But we come across names – by accident, by obligation.

Notes

Constellations

1 Massimo Cacciari, *Icone della legge*, p. 54.
2 This dialogue has been initiated by Karl-Otto Apel. We find in Wittgenstein and Heidegger 'a questioning of the model of thought which has dominated the logic of language since Aristotle. According to this model, words in language a "meaning" because they "designate" something. Going back to the origin of this schema of representation, we could say that words are supposed to be "names" for "existing things" or "objects".' Karl-Otto Apel, 'Wittgeinstein und Heidegger', p. 376.
3 The first and last chapters of this book were presented to Jacques Derrida's seminar. The second is a contribution to a colloquium on translation which took place in September 1987 in Céret, organised by Charles Alunni and the Collège International de Philosophie. The third text, finally, was written especially for this book.

I would like to thank Giorgio Agamben, Ginevra Bompiani, Silvia Bovenschen, Philippe Lacoue-Labarthe, Jean-Luc Nancy and Hugo Santiago.

I   On the Path towards Sacred Names

4 *Translator's note*: the original title is '*Du chemin vers les noms sacrés*'. '*Du chemin*' can also mean 'It's quite a long way' (to get to the sacred names)!
5 Martin Heidegger, *What Is Called Thinking?*, p. 117.
6 Karl Löwith, 'Heidegger and Rosenzweig. Ein Nachtrag zu "Sein und Zeit",' in *Heidegger. Denker in Dürftiger Zeit*, p. 75.

7 Karl Löwith, *My Life in Germany Before and After 1933: A Report*, p. 28.

8 Löwith, 'Ein Nachtrag', p. 78

9 Franz Rosenzweig, *The Star of Redemption*, p. 411.

10 Martin Heidegger, 'The Want of Sacred names', p. 266.

11 *Ibid.* p. 264.

12 Rosenzweig, *The Star*, p. 379.

13 *Ibid.* p. 383.

14 *Ibid.* p. 336.

15 *Ibid.* p. 305.

16 *Ibid.* p. 331.

17 *Ibid.* p. 328. Square brackets from the translator of *The Star*.

18 *Ibid.* p. 415.

19 *Ibid.* p. 405.

20 *Ibid.* p. 302.

21 Georg Friedrich Wilhelm Hegel, *The Science of Logic*, p. 127.

22 Rosenzweig, *The Star*, p. 329.

23 Max Horkheimer, *Gesammelte Schriften*, vol. 12, pp. 263–4.

24 Rosenzweig, *The Star*, pp. 407, 408.

25 *Ibid.* p. 408.

26 In a completely different context, Ginevra Bompiani writes: 'Waiting is the outward leg of the journey from the place of one's birth, outside of oneself, seeking that which the place already contained, and which will permit a return [...] The most proper calls man out of himself, out of the place of his birth.' Ginevra Bompiani, *L'attesa*, pp. 21–2.

27 Rosenzweig, *The Star*, p. 336.

28 *Ibid*, p. 337.

29 *Ibid.* p. 338.

30 *Ibid.*

31 *Ibid.* p. 339.

32 'The epoch is like a thing.'

33 Rosenzweig, *The Star*, p. 339.

34 *Ibid.*

35 *Ibid.* p. 340.

36 *Ibid.* p. 339.

37 *Ibid.*

38 Martin Heidegger, *Discourse on Thinking*, p. 80.

39 Martin Heidegger, *The Principle of Reason*, p. 63.
40 Martin Heidegger, *Nietzsche*, vol. IV, p. 120. Let us try to reconstruct the argument for the non-representational essence of thought. In the dialogue on *Gelassenheit*, i.e. in a discussion whose aim is releasement, the professor says that in order to discover the essence of man, we must turn away from man and avoid fixing our gaze on him. In his essence, man is a being that thinks. But we must not pay too much attention to thought, to its horizon, if we want to think the essential character of this essence. We must free ourselves from the horizon of thought, from the horizon that, from a Kantian perspective, is always created by the synthesising activity of the transcendental imagination. We can sum up the argument schematically: we must look for the essence of something in a 'place', in a 'site' which is not the site of that which is essential, of what has an essence, without for all that being a completely different 'site'. This difference is inscribed in the identity of the *Selbigkeit*, if we hold to the definition given in *Identity and Difference* (p. 24): '*Jedes etwas selber ist ihm selbst zurückgegeben, jedes selber ist dasselbe nämlich für es selbst mit ihm selbst* ['Each thing itself is returned to itself, each itself is the same for itself with itself.'] The essence of thought − of thought as releasement − is what Heidegger names with an archaic German word, *Gegnet*. Its movement, the movement of the *Gegnet*, is a movement of opening which makes the thing − not the object, or *Gegenstand* − surge forth and unfold (*aufgehen*) by giving it duration (*Weile, verweilen* and rest (*Beruhen, ruhen*), by bringing it to rest in itself and to dwell in its rest − which is not s positing. To give rise to is always to make surge forth, make last, let rest; surging forth, lasting, resting, are 'modalities' that point to the event that gives rise, to the giving-rise as event. 'But the *Gegnet* (that-which-regions) and its essence cannot really be two different things − if we may speak here of things at all.' Reply: 'The self (*Selbst*) of the *Gegnet* is presumably its essence (*Wesen*) and *the selfness of its self − of itself (das Selbe ihrer Selbst)*' (*Discourse on Thinking*, p. 86). To think − something essential − is to approach what one thinks and in such a way dwell apart (*fern*) from this 'thing': ' "dwelling"

(*Bleiben*) is the same as "returning" (*Rückkehr*).' The return (*zurück*, *rück-*) is essential to essence as identity. Consequently, the essential character of essence is its approaching alterity, its difference; it is not simply essence, it is not essence in the sense of *Einerlei*, of that which, being simply the same, makes no difference; the essential is the movement which as a spacing that gathers, as essence of thought, lets the thing itself – and thought – dwell in its proper place by making it come back to this place, to this place which is the place, the gathering of a *Selbigkeit* marked by a spacing. We can read the *Gespräch* as a transcription of the saying of Parmenides. It is as if *Gegnet*, the essence of thought, of releasement, the essential of the essence of man, were already its own essence, essence itself, as if its movement were essence determined on the basis of identity, on the basis of *Selbigkeit*. If we think, we always think the essential; that is to say, we let ourselves be carried by the essential movement of the *Gegnet*, by essence. To think is always – and not only when we think the fact of thinking, the essence of man – to do something other than think, something other which is not something else; it is to distract ourselves without for that renouncing thought; to think is to release thought – horizontal and transcendental – without releasing releasement, in other words: not permitting what is released to be recuperated by a self-reflection which would already suppose identity, the identical repetition of an 'I think', and also not permitting thought to become pure indifference. This double precaution, this double attention to distraction, shows that the man who thinks exposes himself to the reappropriation and loss of the difference which constitutes identity. Driven by his wish to found thought on principles, Kant returns to a 'natural disposition' (*Naturanlage*) of man. Heidegger, whose concern is to destroy or deconstruct the axiom of the *animal rationale* while continuing to think on the basis of the identification of human essence with thought, underlines the importance of the Kantian conception of representation. This contains, at its heart, the identity of thought and will: 'Thinking, understood in the traditional way, as re-presenting is a kind of willing [...] Thinking is willing, and willing is thinking [*Denken ist Wollen und Wollen ist Denken*]' (*Discourse on Thinking*, pp. 58–9). If thinking is not essential to the essence of man (*Wegsehen vom Denken*), then the necessity of thinking without thinking, of thinking what thinking without thinking means, of thinking the double attention that this distraction prescribes, translates itself into the necessity of thinking a will of non-will: 'And that is why, in answer to your question as to what I really wanted from our meditation on the nature of thinking, I replied: I want non-willing [*Eich will das Nicht-Wallen*]' (*Ibid.* p. 59). In *Heidegger, Art and Politics: The Fiction of the Political*, Philippe Lacoue-Labarthe invokes in his turn a will of non-will, a willing and a not-willing, a non-pretension to willing and wanting: 'What then does this modesty mean, this claim not to be philosophising? This perhaps: no longer wanting philosophy, and wanting nothing other ... It is precisely the voluntaristic *habitus* that we must renounce' (pp. 4–5). (Lyotard: "The pain of thinking isn't a symptom, coming from outside to inscribe itself on the mind instead of in its true place. It is thought itself resolving to be irresolute, deciding to be patient, wanting not to want, wanting, precisely, not to want to produce a meaning in place of what must be signified." *The Inhuman: Reflections on Time*, p. 19). This reiteration of the requirement which expresses the essential of human essence brings our attention back to the paradoxical appearance of a proposition of the form *wanting not to want* or *willing not to will*. It vacillates, it leads us to understand that there is an essential incertitude or indecision. *Willing not to will*: an affirming of the will and, at the same time, for the time it takes to return to the essential, a desisting from the will. *Willing not to will* signifies not wanting to will, and wanting nothing which is not of the order of the will, nothing which could be an object outside of this order. Willing, willing philosophy or thought, can always be a form of non-willing; on the other hand, non-willing can be a form of willing. The scholar insists on the equivocal character of the formulation: "Non-willing, for one thing, means a willing in such a way as to involve negation, be it even in the sense of a negation which is directed at willing and renounces it. Non-willing means, therefore, willingly to renounce willing. And the term non-willing means, further, what remains absolutely outside any kind of will" (*Discourse on Thinking*, p. 59). To think and, while thinking, to cross the territory of the will; to think and to start out from the extenuation of the will, or its more or less negative negation; to think and to divest thought of its voluntaristic *habitus*; to think that which does not allow itself to be clothed in this *habitus* and which is thus essential to thought – that is the concern of the *Erörterung*.

41 Rosenzweig, *The Star*, pp. 341–2.

42 *Ibid.* p. 366.

43 *Ibid.* p. 343.

44 *Ibid.* p. 342.

45 *Ibid.* pp. 413–14.

46 *Ibid.* p. 329.

47 *Ibid.* pp. 300–1.

48 Christians, says Horkheimer, attested to their religion by doing the opposite of what they should have done. Persecution and murder were the response to the profession of Jewish faith – to the attestation to God and his people. Could the Jews do nothing other than attest to their religion? Couldn't they do what the Christians did? Does Christian hatred go back to the distinction between discourse and generation, this distinction that Rosenzweig claims to be the origin of Christianity? Horkheimer writes: "To save themselves [the jews] had to either deny their God or form themselves into a State. These two options mean the loss of Judaism: one implies that the Jews disappear, being no longer present in the world, the other that they fall into the inevitable nationalism of the others. Israel" (*Gesammelte Schriften*, vol. 14, pp. 314–15). To save themselves, the Jews must dissociate the indissociable: attestation.

49 Rosenzweig, *The Star*, pp. 295.

50 Martin, Heidegger, *Being and Time*, p. 318 (§ 56).

51 Walter Benjamin, 'The Metaphysics of Youth', in *Walter Benjamin: Selected Writings*, vol. 1.

52 Rosenzweig, *The Star*, pp. 295–6.

53 *Ibid*, p. 372.

54 *Translator's note. garder*, the word used in the original, has a

number of related meanings, principally 'to hold' and 'to keep'. The one most appropriate to the context has been used in the translation, but both should be kept in mind when one or the other is used. There is also a word-play with *garder* and *regarder* ('to look', 'to glance') throughout the section. In '*ce sont les noms qui nous gardent et nous regardent*', *ce qui nous regarde* means both 'what watches us' and 'what concerns us'.

55 And in solitude: 'The purest solitude, which is affected by neither the desire for independence nor the feeling of being isolated, solitude accepted in releasement receives the gift of the distant gaze which gives it its support.' Marí Zambrano, *Claros del bosque*, p. 132.

56 Jacques Derrida, *The Postcard*, p. 118.

57 'The having-been, on the contrary, continues to be, we ourselves are that in some way to the extent that, placing it before us, safeguarding it and holding it before us, or again pushing it away and wanting to forget it, we make it penetrate into our *Da-sein*. The shadows of those who were visit us anew, come to us, are to come.' Martin Heidegger, 'Hölderlins Hymnen "Germanien" and "Der Rhein" ', in *Gesamtausgabe*, vol. 39, p. 108.

58 Perhaps it is in this sense that we should understand what Werner Hamacher says about 'correspondence' in Benjamin's thinking: 'But just as no-one can correspond to oneself, no-one can correspond to one's own death.' Hamacher, 'The Word "*Wolke*" – If It Is One', in *Benjamin's Ground: New Readings of Walter Benjamin*, p. 171.

59 Rosenzweig, *The Star*, p. 186.

60 *Ibid.* pp. 273–4.

61 *Ibid.* p. 423.

62 *Ibid.* pp. 187–8.

63 Part One, Book Three of *The Star*.

64 Martin Heidegger, 'The Self-assertion of the German University', in *Review of Metaphysics*, p. 475.

65 Jacques Derrida, *Of Spirit*: Heidegger and the Question, Chapter 6, p. 47 onwards.

66 Jacques Derrida, 'La langue et le discours de la méthode', in *Recherches sur la philosophie et le langage*, vol. 3, 1983, pp. 35–51.

67 Philippe Lacoue-Labarthe, *La poésie comme expérience*, p. 149.

68 Heidegger, 'The Want', p. 266.

69 Martin Heidegger, 'Gedachtes', in *Philosophy Today*, pp. 286–90.

70 Heidegger, 'Zu einem Vors von Mörike', in *Denkerfahrungen*, p. 51.

71 Martin Heidegger, 'Réponse à Max Kommerell', letter of 5 August 1942, in *Philosophie*, p. 16. ('What is taking place here, is an exposure of a thought to a poet, an exposure which goes as far as posing that which is opposed. Is this arbitrary or supreme liberty?')

72 Martin Heidegger, *On the Way to Language*, p. 26. '*Dasein* has become a stranger to its own historical essence, to its mission and its task. Alienated from itself, it remains without determination, indeterminable and as such "without interpretation"' (*deutungslos*). Determination is lacking because the fundamental tone of the insertion into essential conflicts is unable to determine the tone; it is without pain, that is to say without the fundamental form of spiritual knowledge, and that is why "*without pain are we*". Where the cracks in Being do not open themselves up, thereby giving the tone, there is no urgency of having to name, to say; and that is why "*we have almost forgotten language in foreign countries*". We are a sign (*Zeichen*), a frozen signal or hint (*Wink*), a signal or hint forgotten by the gods, as it were' (Heidegger, 'Hölderlins Hymnen "Germanien" und "Der Rhein"', p. 135). A *Zeichen* is thus a forgotten *Wink*, the forgetting of language which is, for man, the forgetting of his essence. The experience of language is always the experience of distress and necessity, of a conflict which is at the origin of this distress and this necessity.

73 Heidegger, *On the Way*, p. 27.

74 Heidegger, 'Hölderlins Hymnen "Germanien" und "Der Rhein"', p. 32.

75 Martin Heidegger, 'Das Gedicht', in *Erläuterungen zu Hölderlins Dichtung*, p. 188.

76 Heidegger, 'Hölderlins Hymnen "Germanien" und "Der Rhein"', p. 45.

77 Heidegger, *The Principle of Reason*, p. 54.

II *Translating the Thing*

78 Jacques Derrida, 'The *Retrait* of Metaphor' in *Enclitic*, p. 30.
79 Walter Benjamin, 'On Language in General and the Language of Man', in *One-Way Street and Other Writings*, p. 118.
80 *Ibid.*
81 *Ibid.* p. 92.
82 *Ibid.* p. 117.
83 *Ibid.* p. 110.
84 Paul de Man, 'Conclusions: Walter Benjamin's "Task of the Translator"', in *The Resistance to Theory*, p. 80.
85 Walter Benjamin, 'Doctrine of the Similar', in *New German Critique*, p. 65.
86 Benjamin, 'On Language', p. 107.
87 *Ibid.* p. 108.
88 *Ibid.*
89 *Ibid.*
90 *Ibid.* p. 112.
91 *Ibid.* p. 108.
92 *Ibid.* p. 117.
93 *Ibid.* pp. 112–13.
94 *Ibid.* p. 112.
95 Walter Benjamin, 'On the Mimetic Faculty', in *One-Way Street and Other Writings*, p. 162.
96 Benjamin, 'On Language', p. 118.
97 *Ibid.*
98 Heidegger, *What Is Called Thinking?*, p. 232.
99 *Ibid.* p. 138.
100 Jean-Luc Nancy, 'Of Divine Places', in *The Inoperative Community*, p. 115.
101 Heidegger, *What Is Called Thinking?*, p. 120.
102 Heidegger, *On the Way to Thinking*, p. 123.

III *Over-naming and melancholy*

103 Walter Benjamin, 'Franz Kafka: On the Tenth Anniversary of His Death', in *Illuminations*, p. 136.

104 Friedrich Wilhelm Joseph Schelling, *Of Human Freedom*, p. 79.

105 Theodor W. Adorno, *Kierkegaard: Construction of the Aesthetic*, p. 62. In the passage of the 'Philosophy of Religion' which he devotes to the religion of the sublime, Hegel claims that the melancholy of nature – of all that is natural – is the result of a failure to understand death. For the mind which has passed through death there is no – natural – melancholy.

106 Heidegger, 'Hölderlins Hymnen "Germanien" and "Der Rhein"', p. 81.

107 Martin Heidegger, *Schelling's Treatise on the Essence of Human Freedom*, p. 160.

108 Martin Heidegger, *Introduction to Metaphysics*, pp. 152–3.

109 Walter Benjamin, 'Two Poems by Friedrich Hölderlin', in *Selected Writings*, p. 32. Doubtless a rigorous analysis of the structure of *Dasein* – we find it in Jean-Luc Nancy's work on freedom – would show that the question of melancholy – and of denomination – is displaced by this very structure. This displacement may come close to what Benjamin is thinking of when he speaks of the object's sadness, which would originate in a universal over-naming – the subject of this text. But if there is anything equivocal, it is because voluntarism (the will to appear to oneself) which, in Heidegger, is linked to the theme of the *Volk* and so to the themes of foundation and denomination, makes a 'metaphysical' interpretation of melancholy possible; we must distinguish voluntarism from 'to will willing' in the sense of an effective exposition 'to existing effectivity (which is nothing else than an exposing effectivity)'. (See Jean-Luc Nancy, *The Experience of Liberty*, p. 28; about the problem of creation see pp. 83–6.)

110 Giorgio Agamben, *Stanzas*, p. 20.

111 Benjamin, 'On Language', p. 121.

112 *Ibid.*

113 *Ibid.*

114 *Ibid.*

115 Theodor W. Adorno, *Minima Moralia*, §72, p. 112.

116 Rosenzweig, *The Star*, p. 244.

117 Heidegger, *Discourse on Thinking*, p. 82.

118 Benjamin, 'On Language', p. 121.
119 *Ibid.* pp. 121–2.
120 *Ibid.* p. 120.
121 *Ibid.* p. 122.
122 *Ibid.* p. 123.
123 Walter Benjamin, *The Origin of German Tragic Drama*, pp. 183–4.
124 *Ibid.* p. 182.
125 Paul de Man, *Allegories of Reading*, p. 74.
126 Benjamin, *The Origin*, pp. 224–5.
127 *Ibid.* p. 109.
128 *Ibid.* pp. 139–40.
129 Benjamin, 'On Language', p. 122.
130 These two texts were translated into French by Jean-Luc Nancy and Philippe Lacoue-Labarthe.
131 Walter Benjamin, 'The Role of Language in *Trauerspiel* and Tragedy' in *Selected Writings*, p. 59.
132 Benjamin, 'On Language', p. 121.
133 *Ibid.* p. 119.
134 *Ibid.* p. 120.
135 *Ibid.*
136 Walter Benjamin 'For a Critique of Mythical Violence', in *One-Way Street and Other Writings*, pp. 150–1.
137 'It is only on the limit or at a frontier that the time comes for decisions to be taken; decisions actually always decide about limits or frontiers and the absence of limits or frontiers.' Heidegger, 'Hölderlins Hymnen "Germanien" und "Der Rhein"', p. 170.
138 Does Benjamin's essay 'On Language in General and the Language of Man' escape abstraction, judgement, signification? It is perhaps not insignificant to note that Schloem wanted to translate this essay into the language which seems proper to it – Hebrew, the originary language (*Ursprache*). Apparently, Benjamin did not use this expression without irony, at least in this context. Is 'On Language ...' a text destined not to be heard in German? Can someone who speaks only German hear and understand it? Did Benjamin, who never learned Hebrew, translate a Hebrew text without translating it? We are reminded here of Heidegger and his invention of a Greek phrase ... In so

far as the attempt to approach the *Urspracge*, what is *ursprachlich* in Hebrew, can be considered as an attempt to approach prayer – Rosenzweig says that the Jew speaks the sacred language only when he addresses God – the dimension of the text is no longer that of abstraction. Benjamin's essay is necessarily a participant in both: abstraction and prayer. It cannot be otherwise for a text whose starting point is not a hypothesis but a particular experience linked to a truth which escapes being presented as a hypothesis. That is the explanation of the reactions Benjamin can provoke: it is said that his thought is heavily dogmatic and unverifiable, that his style is apodictic and non-discursive, even authoritarian. What if these effects were inevitable when one tries to think the event of the gift?

139 Benjamin, 'The Role'.
140 Walter Benjamin, '*Trauerspiel* and Tragedy', in *Selected Writings*, pp. 55–6.
141 *Ibid.* p. 57.
142 Aristotle, *The Man of Genius and Melancholy* (*Problems*, Book XXX), 'Problems Connected with Practical Wisdom, Intelligence, and Wisdom', p. 1.
143 Benjamin, 'The Role', p. 60.
144 *Ibid.* p. 61.
145 *Ibid.* p. 60.
146 *Ibid.* p. 61.
147 Theodor W. Adorno, 'Music and Language: A Fragment', in *Quasi una Fantasia*, pp. 2–3.
148 Theodor W. Adorno, 'Notes on Philosophical Thinking', in *Critical Models: Interventions and Catchwords*, pp. 131–2.
149 Benjamin, *The Origin*, p. 137.
150 Heidegger, 'Hölderlins Hymnen "Germanien" und "Der Rhein"', p. 94.
151 Walter Benjamin, 'Berliner Kindheit', in *Gesammelte Schriften*, pp. 303–4. The piece on 'The Little Hunchback' ends with a demand for a prayer: 'I imagine that this "entire life" which people say flashes before the eyes of the dying is made up of pictures like those the Little Hunchback has of all of us. They flash by at great speed, like the little books with tight bindings that were once the precursors of moving pictures. The thumb, pressing gently, would

move across the side of the little books. Then, for a few seconds, pictures would appear which could not be distinguished from one another. The unfolding of these pictures allowed one to see the boxer at work or the swimmer battling against the waves. The Little Hunchback also has pictures of me. He saw me in my hiding place, in front of the otter's cage on winter mornings and in front of the telephone in the back of the house, on the crest of the Brasserie with the butterflies and on the ice rink as the fanfare sounded, in front of the sewing box and leaning over my drawer, at Blumeshof and when I was sick in bed, at Glienicke and at the train station. Now he has finished his work. Even so his voice, which reminds me of the song of the mantle of the gas lamp, still murmurs these words to me beyond the threshold of the century: "O my dear child, please / Pray for the Little Hunchback, too" ' (*Ibid.* p. 304). This passage seems to resonate with another, found at the end of the tenth thesis on the storyteller. 'It is, however, characteristic that not only a man's knowledge or wisdom, but above all his real life, and this is the stuff that stories are made of − first assumes transmissible form at the moment of his death. Just as a sequence of images is set in motion inside a man as his life comes to an end unfolding the views of himself under which he has encountered himself without being aware of it − suddenly in his expressions and looks the unforgettable emerges and imparts to everything that concerned him that authority which even the poorest wretch who is dying possesses for the living around him. This authority is at the very source of the story' ('The Storyteller', in *Illuminations*, p. 94). The little hunchback has finished his work. Why? Because the child has become an adult. Now the one who was a child is entirely traversed by language. Language perpetuates the presence of the little hunchback, it is the omnipresence that makes his previous and always surprising presence superfluous. But both his previous presence and his present omnipresence result from a withdrawal. We remember the 'bringer of forgetfulness' (*Bote des Vergessens*), as Benjamin calls the little hunchback in a fragment, through language. Adorno bears witness to this. "One evening in a mood of helpless sadness, I caught myself using a ridiculously wrong subjunctive form of a verb that was itself not entirely correct German, being part of the dialect of my native town. I had not heard, let alone used, this endearing misconstruction since my first years at school. Melancholy, drawing me irresistibly into the abyss of childhood, awakened this old, impotently yearning sound in its depth. Language had sent back to me like an echo the humiliation which unhappiness had inflicted on me in forgetting who I am" (*Minima moralia*, pp. 110–11). The little hunchback is recognised just as much through the surprise felt when language fails – which is itself always the language of over-naming – as in the gift of storytelling. One encounters oneself without knowing it. One touches the stuff of life, one experiences the unforgettable – the gift – which gives itself as the forgetting of a gift. But to undergo such an experience is always to reach a limit. The one who dies transmits nothing because he passes into the transmissible. The one who tells a story turns back and never arrives. What happens next? That is the question of storytelling.

IV Apparitions

152 Theodor W. Adorno, 'The Handle, the Pot and Early Experience', in *Notes to Literature*, vol. 1, p. 211.
153 Adorno, *Minima Moralia*, pp. 110–11 (see note 151 above).
154 Benjamin, 'On Language', p. 116.
155 *Ibid*. p. 115.
156 *Ibid*.
157 *Ibid*. p. 114.
158 *Ibid*. pp. 115–16.
159 *Ibid*. p. 118.
160 *Ibid*. p. 116.
161 Philo of Alexandria, 'De mutatione nominum', in *Philo of Alexandria: The Contemplative life*, in 'The Giants and Selections', p. 142.
162 Heidegger, *On the Way to Language*, p. 154.
163 Emile Benveniste, *Problèmes de linguistique générale*, vol. II, p. 200.

164 Walter Benjamin, 'Theologico-political Fragment', in *One-Way Street and Other Writings*, p. 156.

165 Giorgio Agamben, 'Langue et histoire', in *Walter Benjamin*, p. 795.

166 It is true that any promise inevitably reduces the surprise of the gift (this is why Juan David García Bacca claims that you cannot promise a gift; cf. *Tres ejercicios filosófico-literarios de economía*, p. 31). However, we cannot completely separate the promise from a surprise. A promise is always surprising and improbable. It is not erased when it has been kept: what happens is never what had been promised and is not without promise. Surprise is the memory of a promise.

167 The 'logic' of the gift also ruins any speculation which seeks to benefit from forgetting. For forgetting that 'this happens' – absolutely forgetting the gift, which is thus the absolute gift – erases, by erasing the gift itself, all possibility of receiving a benefit; that is to say, of making the gift return, absolutely.

168 Benjamin, 'Theologico-political Fragment', p. 154.

169 Philippe Lacoue-Labarthe, 'Poétique et politique', in *L'imitation des Modernes*, p. 199. My italics, A.G.D.

170 *Translator's Note*: in the title and throughout this section there is a play on the similarity of *avenir* ('future') and *à venir* ('yet to come').

171 Gershom Scholem, 'Toward an Understanding of the Messianic Idea in Judaism', in *The Messianic Idea in Judaism*, p. 11.

172 Baruch de Spinoza. *Tractatus Theologico-Politicus*, pp. 66–7.

173 Walter Benjamin, 'Theses on the Philosophy of History', in *Illuminations*, p. 257.

174 Benjamin, 'Theologico-political fragment', p. 155.

175 If the future is the coming of the other, the other yet to come, and if this future does not let itself be anticipated, if the promise and the memory of the other are absolutely original, then the other is always the one who can come and who comes at any moment, *who is already there*.

176 Jean-François Lyotard, *The Differend*, p. 88.

177 Theodor W. Adorno, *Aesthetic Theory*, p. 79.

178 *Ibid.* p. 83.

179 *Ibid.* p. 85.

180 *Ibid.* p. 82.
181 *Ibid.*
182 *Ibid.* p. 78.
183 *Ibid.* p. 83.
184 *Ibid.* p. 80.
185 Benjamin, 'Theologico-political Fragment', p. 155.
186 Friedrich Nietzsche, *On The Genealogy of Morality*, p. 39. Werner Hamacher reads this passage differently. He shows that the relationship the will maintains with itself and establishes through memory and promise consists of an alteration because it consists of an interpretation of will as will. Will is a given word. (Cf. Werner Hamacher, 'The Promise of Interpretation: Remarks on the Hermeneutic Imperative in Kant and Nietzsche', in *Premises: Essays on Philosophy and Literature from Kant to Celan*, pp. 112–14.)
187 Jacques Derrida, *Mémoires: for Paul de Man*, p. 150.
188 Adorno, *Aesthetic Theory*, p. 84.
189 Theodor W. Adorno, *Prisms*, p. 34.
190 Philippe Lacoue-Labarthe, 'The Response of Ulysses', in *Who Comes After the Subject?*
191 Lyotard, *The Differend*, p. 88.
192 Emmanual Levinas, 'The Name of God According to a Few Talmudic Texts', in *Beyond the Verse*, p. 122.
193 Benjamin, 'On Language', pp. 119–20. My italics, A.G.D.
194 'Doesn't Soloviel, the cabbalist, say that these two voices, that of God which we must not name and that of unnameable evil, are so absolutely alike that the difference between them is like the sound of a raindrop in the ocean?' (George Steiner, *Comment taire?*, p. 14.)
195 Theodor W. Adorno, *Negative Dialectics*, p. 365.
196 Immanuel Kant, *Critique of Judgement*, Part I, Book II, pp. 127–8.
197 *Ibid.* p. 128.
198 Jacques Derrida, 'Before the law', in *Kafka and the Contemporary Critical Performance: Centenary Readings*, p. 141.
199 Peter Szondi, 'Durch die Enge geführt', in *Celan-Studien*, pp. 102–3.
200 Max Horkheimer and Theodor W. Adorno, *The Dialectic of Enlightenment*, p. 23.

201 Hermann Cohen, *Die Religion der Vernunft aus den Quellen des Judentums*, p. 403.
202 Sigmund Freud, *Moses and Monotheism*, pp. 179–80, 185–6.
203 Lyotard, *The Differend*, pp. 57–8.
204 Philippe Lacoue-Labarthe and Jean-Luc Nancy (eds), *Les fins de l'homme. A partir du travail de Jacques Derrida*, p. 311.
205 Adorno, *Negative Dialectics*, p. 52.
206 Theodor W. Adorno, 'Notiz öber Namen', in *Gesammelte Schriften*, vol. 20.2. Like Adorno, Heidegger links names with destiny. In his analysis of the poem '*Das Wort*' he says that the poet needs names because names are the words which show the thing and make representation possible: they are *die darstellenden Worte* and 'they present what is already to representational thinking': "The poet himself composes in virtue of the claim to the names. In order to reach them, he must first in his journeys attain to that place where his claim finds the required fulfilment. This happens at his country's strand. The strand bounds, it arrests, limits and circumscribes the poet's secure sojourn. The bourn, the well from which the twilit norn, the ancient goddess of fate, draws up the names is at the edge of the poet's land – or is the edge itself the well? With these names she gives the poet those words which he, confidently and sure of himself, awaits as the portrayal of what he believes to be that which is. The poet's claim to the rule of his Saying is confirmed. The flourishing and shining of his poetry become presence. The poet is sure of his word, and just as fully in command of it" (*On the Way to Language*, pp. 144–5). But there is one word that the Norn withholds: this withdrawal of the name, this lack (*Ausbleiben des Namens*), puts an end to the poet's journey to the Norn's well. 'For by this new experience the poet has caught sight of a different rule of the word, although in a veiled manner' (*Ibid*. p. 146). The word, the missing word, is the word of the word. So the poet who experiences the withdrawal of the name abandons representation and abandons himself to 'the word's hidden essence which, invisibly in its Saying and even already in what is unsaid, extends to us the thing as thing' (*Ibid*. p. 154). The withdrawal of the name, its essential illegibility, leads us away from destiny – as representation.

207 Adorno, *Negative Dialectics*, p. 362.

208 *Ibid.* pp. 362–3.

209 Theodor W. Adorno, 'On Lyric Poetry and Society', in *Notes to Literature*, vol. 1, p. 53.

210 A dossier containing all the texts where Adorno has raised and raised again the question of poetry after Auschwitz has been collated by Petra Kiedaisch and was published in 1995; see *Lyrik nach Auschwitz? Adorno und die Dichet.*

211 Theodor W. Adorno, 'Commitment', in *Notes to Literature*, vol. 2, pp. 87–8.

212 Lacoue-Labarthe, *La poésie comme expérience*, p. 18. What does 'banality' mean 'after Auschwitz'? There are several answers. (1) Everything has become unbearably banal compared with the past of that which came before Auschwitz. (2) Everything has become unbearably banal compared with the incommensurable reality of Auschwitz. (3) Nothing is more banal than the necessity and its affirmation. We are from now on condemned to repeat: 'Everything has become banal . . .' and this repetition itself is not exempt from banality. 'The lack of possibility means that everything has become either a necessity or a banality for us', writes Kierkegaard. The affirmation of banality – necessity – is already a revocation, otherwise Adorno could not have written a text entitled 'After Auschwitz'. As soon as we affirm the necessity of banality – this expression is a pleonasm – we do not simply negate possibility, we also deny that we have already acknowledged it. We seem to be quite able to stand the banality we call unbearable. Perhaps this banality, made of its own repeated affirmation, should have a different name: it is rather a fault, given that doing wrong to the only thought of which we think that we can affirm the 'impossible possibility' – thought 'after Auschwitz' – means making oneself guilty, even if such wrongdoing is inevitable. (4) The time described by the expression 'after Auschwitz' – our time – is characterised by the banality of evil Hannah Arendt speaks of when writing about Eichmann: "He was not stupid. It was sheer thoughtlessness – something by no means identical with stupidity – that predisposed him to become one of the greatest criminals of his period. And if this is "banal" and

even funny, if with the best will in the world one cannot extract any diabolical or demonic profundity from Eichmann, that is still far from calling it commonplace [...] That such remoteness from reality and such thoughtlessness can wreak more havoc than all the evil instincts taken together which, perhaps, are inherent in man – that was, in fact, the lesson one could learn in Jerusalem. But it was a lesson, neither an explanation of the phenomenon nor a theory about it" (Hannah Arendt, *Eichmann in Jerusalem: A Report on the Banality of Evil*, pp. 287–8).

213 Alfred Schmidt, 'Begriff des Materialismus bei Adorno' ['The Concept of Materialism in Adorno'], in *Adorno-Konferenz 1983*, p. 27.

214 Adorno, *Negative Dialectics*, p. 204.

215 Theodor W. Adorno, *Philosophische Terminologie*, vol. II, p. 181.

216 Adorno, *Negative Dialectics*, p. 207.

217 *Ibid.* p. 364 Jean-Luc Nancy states: 'Auschwitz signified the death of birth and death, their conversion into an infinite abstraction, the negation of existence' (*The Experience of Freedom*, p. 122). The 'infinite abstraction' of death must not be confused with this other abstraction which is the root of all – 'metaphysical' – forms of despair, if we go along with Kierkegaard's analysis. It consists of the isolation of an element inherent to the constitution of the I. Dying without dying, dying death – this is the formula that summarises the essence of despair for Kierkegaard: "It is in this last sense that despair is the sickness unto death, this agonising contradiction, this sickness in the self, everlastingly to die, to die and yet not to die, to die the death. For dying means that it is all over, but dying the death means to live to experience death; and if for a single instant this experience is possible, it is tantamount to experiencing it forever [...] The dying of despair transforms itself continually into a living. This despairing man cannot die; no more than "the dagger can slay thoughts" can despair consume the eternal thing, the self, which is the ground of despair, whose worm dieth not and whose fire is not quenched." Further on, Kierkegaard writes: 'If there were nothing eternal in man, he could not despair; but if despair

could consume his self, there would still be no despair' *The Sickness Unto Death*, pp. 25–6, 30). 'Auschwitz' has destroyed despair and its dialectic. For despair always presupposes the support of an indestructible I. Doesn't the 'coldness' Adorno speaks of – we still live after Auschwitz – show this impossibility of despairing?

218 Maurice Blanchot, 'After the Fact', in *Vicious Circles: Two Fictions*, pp. 68–9.

219 Adorno, *Negative Dialectics*, p. 365.

220 Heidegger, 'Hölderlins Hymne Andenken', in *Gesamtausgabe*, p. 286.

221 Theodor W. Adorno, *Mahler*, p. 29.

222 Jean-Luc Nancy, 'The Inoperative Community', in *The Inoperative Community*, p. 24.

223 Adorno, *Negative Dialectics*, pp. 391–2.

224 Jacques Derrida, *Glas*, p. 7. Adorno is aware of this function of the name: "In a certain sense, I ought to have been able to deduce Fascism from the memories of my childhood. As a conqueror dispatches envoys to the remotest provinces, Fascism had sent its advance guard there long before it marched in: my schoolfellows. If the bourgeois class has from time immemorial nurtured the dream of a brutal national community, of oppression of all by all, then children already equipped with names like Horst and Jürgen and surnames like Bergenroth, Bojunga and Eckhart enacted the dream before the adults were historically ripe for its realisation" (*Minima Moralia*, p. 192).

225 Adorno, *Aesthetic Theory*, p. 135.

226 Adorno, *Negative Dialectics*, p. 362.

227 Adorno, *Mahler*, p. 154.

228 Walter Benjamin, 'The Work of Art in the Age of Mechanical Reproduction', in *Illuminations*, p. 224.

229 Adorno, *Negative Dialectics*, p. 373.

230 Hannah Arendt, 'Walter Benjamin: 1892–1940' in *Men in Dark Times*, pp. 151–203.

231 We are always disappointed by a revelation. If the revelation – or the apocalypse – disappoints, it is perhaps not because of a mastery which man still lacks. In an essay included in his book *Friendship*, Blanchot says: 'A power that is not in our power, that only points to a possibility

without mastery, a probability – which is, let us say, probable-improbable – that would be our power, a power in us and a power over us, only if we dominated it with certainty' ('The Apocalypse Is Disappointing', p. 106). If a revelation – or an apocalypse – disappoints, it is rather because of the promise: it withdraws when it is fulfilled or kept, when that which is promised comes to pass. What comes to pass is not necessarily something lacking something: it is something which is other. The withdrawal of the promise gives rise to the other while also keeping the possibility open of another coming of the other, thanks to another promise.

232 Hedegger, *Nietzsche*, vol. IV, p. 226.

Bibliography

ADORNO, Theodor W.

Aesthetic Theory, translated by Robert Hullot-Kentor, London: The Athlone Press 1997

'Commitment', in: *Notes to Literature*, volume 2, pp. 76–94

'The Handle, the Pot, and Early Experience', in: *Notes to Literature*, volume 2, pp. 211–19

The Jargon of Authenticity, translated by Knut Tarnowski and Frederic Will, London: Routledge and Kegan Paul 1973

Kierkegaard: Construction of the Aesthetic, translated by Robert Hullot-Kentor, Minneapolis: University of Minnesota Press 1989

Mahler, translated by Edmund Jephcott, Chicago: University of Chicago Press 1992

Minima Moralia, translated by Edmund Jephcott, London: NLB and Verso 1978

'Music and Language: A Fragment', in: *Quasi una Fantasia*, translated by Rodney Livingstone, London: Verso 1992

Negative Dialectics, translated by E. B. Ashton, London: Routledge and Kegan Paul 1990

'Notes on Philosophical Thinking', in: *Critical Models: Interventions and Catchwords*, translated by Henry W. Pickford, New York: Colorado University Press 1997, pp. 127–34

Notes to Literature, volume 1, translated by Shierry Weber Nicholsen, New York: Columbia University Press 1991

Notes to Literature, volume 2, translated by Shierry Weber Nicholson, New York: Columbia University Press 1992

'On Lyric Poetry and Society', in: *Notes to Literature*, volume 1, pp. 37–54

'Notiz über Namen', in: *Gesammelte Schriften*, volume 20.2, Frankfurt am Main: Suhrkamp 1986

Philosophische Terminologie, volume 2, Frankfurt am Main: Suhrkamp 1974
Prisms, translated by Samuel and Shierry Weber, Cambridge, MA: MIT Press 1981

AGAMBEN, Giorgio
'Langue et histoire', in: *Walter Benjamin*, edited by Hans Wisman, Paris: Editions du Cerf 1986
Stanzas, translated by Ronald Martinez, Minneapolis: University of Minnesota Press 1993

APEL, Karl-Otto
'Wittgenstein und Heidegger', in: *Heidegger. Perspektiven zur Deutung seines Werkes*, edited by Otto Pöggeler, Königstein: Athenäum 1984, p. 376

ARENDT, Hannah
Eichmann in Jerusalem: A Report on the Banality of Evil, New York: Penguin Books 1979
'Walter Benjamin: 1892–1940', in: *Men in Dark Times*, Harmondsworth, Mx: Penguin Books 1973, pp. 151–203

ARISTOTLE
The Man of Genius and Melancholy (*Problems*, Book XXX), in: *The Complete Works of Aristotle*, volume 2, Princeton, NJ: Princeton University Press 1984, pp. 1498–1506

BENJAMIN, Walter
Berliner Kindheit ['A Berlin Childhood'], in: *Gesammelte Schriften*, volume IV.1, Frankfurt am Main: Suhrkamp 1972
'Doctrine of the Similar', translated by Knut Tarkowski, in: *New German Critique*, issue 17, 1979, pp. 65–9
'For a Critique of Mythical Violence', in: *One-Way Street and Other Writings*, pp. 132–154
'Franz Kafka: On the Tenth Anniversary of His Death', in: *Illuminations*, pp. 111–140
Illuminations, translated by Harry Zohn, London: Jonathan Cape 1970
'The Metaphysics of Youth', translated by Rodney Living-

stone, in: *Walter Benjamin: Selected Writings*, volume 1, pp. 6–17

'On Language in General and the Language of Man', in: *One-Way Street and Other Writings*, pp. 107–23

'On the Mimetic Faculty', in: *One-Way Street and Other Writings*, pp. 160–3

One-Way Street and Other Writings, translated by Edmund Jephcott and Kingsley Shorter, London: NLB and Verso 1979

The Origin of German Tragic Drama, translated by John Osborne, London: NLB and Verso 1977

'The Role of Language in *Trauerspiel* and Tragedy', in: *Selected Writings*, volume 1, pp. 59–61

Selected Writings, volume 1, edited by Marcus Bullock and M. W. Jennings, Cambridge, MA: Harvard University Press 1996

'The Storyteller', in: *Illuminations*, pp. 83–110

'*Trauerspiel* and Tragedy', in: *Selected Writings*, volume 1, pp. 55–8

'Theses on the Philosophy of History', in: *Illuminations*, pp. 255–66

'Theologico-political Fragment', in: *One-Way Street and Other Writings*, pp. 155–6

'Two Poems by Friedrich Hölderlin', translated by Stanley Corngold, in: *Selected Writings,* volume 1, pp. 18–36

'The Work of Art in the Age of Mechanised Reproduction', in: *Illuminations*, pp. 219–54

BENVENISTE, Emile
Problèmes de linguistique générale, Paris: Gallimard 1974

BLANCHOT, Maurice
'After the Fact', in: *Vicious Circles: Two Fictions and 'After the Fact'*, translated by Paul Auster, New York: Station Hill Press 1985, pp. 59–69

'The Apocalypse Is Disappointing', in: *Friendship*, translated by Elizabeth Rottenberg, Stanford: Stanford University Press 1997, pp. 101–8

BOMPIANI, Ginevra
L'attesa, Milan: Feltrinelli 1988

CACCIARI, Massimo
Icone della legge, Milan: Adelphi 1985

COHEN, Hermann
Die Religion der Vernunft aus den Quellen des Judentums, Wiesbaden: Fourier 1988

DERRIDA, Jacques
'Before the Law', translated by Avital Ronell, in: *Kafka and the Contemporary Critical Performance: Centenary Readings*, edited by Alan Udoff, Bloomington: Indiana University Press 1987, pp. 128–49
Glas, translated by John P. Leavey and Richard Rand, Lincoln: University of Nebraska Press 1986
'La langue et le discours de la méthode', in: *Recherches sur la philosophie et le langage*, volume 3, Grenoble 1983, pp. 35–51
Mémoires: for Paul de Man, translated by Cecile Lindsay, Jonathan Culler and Eduardo Cadava, New York: Columbia University Press 1986
Of Spirit: Heidegger and the Question, translated by Geoffrey Bennington and Rachel Bowlby, Chicago: University of Chicago Press 1989
The Postcard, translated by Alan Bass, Chicago: University of Chicago Press 1987
'The *Retrait* of Metaphor', in: *Enclitic*, volume 2, no. 2, 1978, pp. 5–33

FREUD, Sigmund
Moses and Monotheism, translated by Katherine Jones, London: Hogarth Press 1939

GARCIA BACCA, Juan David
Tres ejercicios filosófico-literarios de economía, Barcelona: Anthropos 1983

HAMACHER, Werner
'The Promise of Interpretation: Remarks on the Hermeneutic Imperative in Kant and Nietzsche', translated by Peter Fenves, in: *Premises: Essays on Philosophy and Literature from Kant to Celan*, Cambridge, MA: Harvard University Press 1996, pp. 81–142

'The Word "*Wolke*" – If It Is One', in: *Benjamin's Ground: New Readings of Walter Benjamin*, edited by Rainer Nägele, Detroit, MI: Wayne State University Press 1988, pp. 147–76

HEGEL, Georg Friedrich Wilhelm
The Science of Logic, translated by A. V. Miller, Atlantic Highlands, NJ: Humanities Press International 1995

HEIDEGGER, Martin
Being and Time, translated by John Macquarrie and Edward Robinson, Oxford: Blackwell 1967
Discourse on Thinking [*Gelassenheit*], translated by John M. Anderson and E. Hans Freud, New York: Harper Torchbooks 1966
'Das Gedicht', in: *Erläuterungen zu Hölderlins Dichtung* (Fifth revised edition), Frankfurt am Main: Vitorio Klostermann 1981
'Gedachtes', translated by Keith Hoeller, in: *Philosophy Today*, volume 20, 1976, pp. 286–90
'Hölderlins Hymne Andenken', in: *Gesamtausgabe*, volume 52, Frankfurt am Main: Vitorio Klostermann 1982
'Hölderlins Hymnen "Germanien" und "Der Rhein"', in: *Gesamtausgabe*, volume 39, Frankfurt am Main: Vitorio Klostermann 1980
Identity and Difference, translated by Joan Stambaugh, New York: Harper Torchbooks 1974
Introduction to Metaphysics, translated by Ralph Manheim, New Haven, CT: Yale University Press 1956
Nietzsche, volume IV, translated by Frank A. Capuzzi, edited by David Farrell Krell, New York: Harper and Row 1982
On the Way to Language, New York: Harper and Row 1971
The Principle of Reason, translated by Reginald Lilly, Bloomington: Indiana University Press 1991
'Réponse à Max Kommerell' (letter written on 4 August 1942), in: *Philosophie*, volume 16, Paris 1983
Schelling's Treatise on the Essence of Human Freedom, translated by Joan Stambough, Athens: Ohio University Press 1989
'The Self-assertion of the German University', translated by Karsten Harries, in: *Review of Metaphysics*, volume 38, pp. 470–80

'The Want of Sacred Names', translated by Bernhard Radloff, in: *Man and World*, volume 18, no. 3, 1985, pp. 261–67
What Is Called Thinking?, translated by Fred Wieck and J. Glenn Gray, New York: Harper and Row 1972
'Words', translated by Joan Stambaugh, in: *On the Way to Language*, pp. 139–56

HORKHEIMER, Max
Gesammelte Schriften, volume 12, edited by Alfred Schmidt and Gunzelin Schmidt-Noerr, Frankfurt am Main: Fischer 1985
Gesammelte Schriften, volume 14 Frankfurt am Main: Fischer 1988

HORKHEIMER, Max and ADORNO, Theodor W.
The Dialectic of Enlightenment, translated by John Cumming, London: Verso 1979

KANT, Immanuel
Critique of Judgement, translated by James Creed Meredith, Oxford: Clarendon Press 1952

KIEDAISCH, Petra
Lyrik nach Auschwitz? Adorno und die Dichter, Stuttgart: Reclam 1995

KIERKEGAARD, Søren
The Sickness Unto Death, translated by Walter Lauries, London: Oxford University Press 1941

LACOUE-LABARTHE, Philippe
Heidegger, Art and Politics: The Fiction of the Political, translated by Chris Turner, Oxford: Blackwell 1990
La poésie comme expérience, Paris: Christian Bourgois 1986
'Poétique et politique', in: *L'imitation des Modernes*, Paris: Galilée 1986
'The Response of Ulysses', translated by Avital Ronell, in: *Who Comes After the Subject?*, edited by Eduardo Cadava, Peter Connor and Jean-Luc Nancy, London: Routledge and Kegan Paul 1991
LACOUE-LABARTHE, Philippe and NANCY, Jean-Luc
Les fins de l'homme. A partir du travail de Jacques Derrida, Paris: Galilée 1981

LEVINAS, Emmanuel
'The Name of God According to a Few Talmudic Texts', in:
Beyond the Verse, translated by Gary D. Mole, London: The
Athlone Press 1994, pp. 116–28

LOWITH, Karl
'Heidegger und Rosenzweig. Ein Nachtrag zu "Sein und
Zeit" ', in: *Heidegger. Denker in dürftiger Zeit*, Stuttgart: Metzler
1985
My Life in Germany Before and After 1933: A Report, translated
by Elizabeth King, London: The Athlone Press 1994

LYOTARD, Jean-François
The Differend, translated by Georges Van Den Abbeele,
Manchester: Manchester University Press 1988
The Inhuman: Reflections on Time, translated by Geoffrey
Bennington and Rachel Bowlby, Cambridge: Polity Press
1991

MAN, Paul de
Allegories of Reading, New Haven, CT: Yale University Press
1979
'Conclusions: Walter Benjamin's "Task of the Translator" ',
in: *The Resistance to Theory*, Minneapolis: Minnesota University
Press 1986

NANCY, Jean-Luc
The Experience of Freedom, translated by Bridget McDonald,
Stanford, CA: Stanford University Press 1993
The Inoperative Community, translated by Peter Connor,
Minneapolis: University of Minnesota Press 1991
'The Inoperative Community', in *The Inoperative Community*
'Of Divine Places', translated by Michael Holland, in: *The
Inoperative Community*
NIETZSCHE, Friedrich
On the Genealogy of Morality, translated by Carol Diethe,
Cambridge: Cambridge University Press 1994

PHILO OF ALEXANDRIA
'De mutatione nominum', in: *Philo of Alexandria: The Contemplative Life,* in 'The Giants and Selections', translated by David Winston, London: SPCK 1981

ROSENZWEIG, Franz
The Star of Redemption, translated by William W. Hallo, London: Routledge and Kegan Paul 1971

SCHELLING, Friedrich Wilhelm Joseph
Of Human Freedom, translated by James Guttman, Chicago: Open Court 1936

SCHMIDT, Alfred
'Begriff des Materialismus bei Adorno', in: *Adorno-Konferenz 1983,* Frankfurt am Main: Suhrkamp 1983

SCHOLEM, Gershom
'Toward an Understanding of the Messianic Idea in Judaism', in: *The Messianic Idea in Judaism,* translated by Michael A. Meyer, New York: Schocken Books 1971, pp. 1–36

SPINOZA, Baruch de
Tractatus Theologico-Politicus, translated by Samuel Shirley, Leiden: E. J. Brill 1989

STEINER, George
Comment taire?, Geneva: Editions Cavaliers Seuls 1987

SZONDI, Peter
'Durch die Enge geführt', in: *Celan-Studien,* Frankfurt am Main: Suhrkamp 1972, pp. 47–111

ZAMBRANO, María
Claros del bosque, Barcelona: Seix Barral 1986

Index